FEARLESS
PERFORMANCE
REVIEWS

FEARLESS PERFORMANCE REVIEWS

COACHING CONVERSATIONS THAT TURN EVERY EMPLOYEE INTO A STAR PLAYER

JEFFREY RUSSELL

AND

LINDA RUSSELL

New York   Chicago   San Francisco   Athens   London
Madrid   Mexico City   Milan   New Delhi
Singapore   Sydney   Toronto

1 2 3 4 5 6 7 8 9 10   DOC/DOC   1 9 8 7 6 5 4 3

ISBN   978-0-07-180472-1
MHID   0-07-180472-2

e-ISBN   978-0-07-180473-8
e-MHID   0-07-180473-0

Library of Congress Cataloging-in-Publication Data

Russell, Jeff (Jeffrey Lee)
   Fearless performance reviews : coaching conversations that turn every employee into a star player / by Jeff Russell and Linda Russell. — 1 Edition.
      pages cm
   ISBN 978-0-07-180472-1 (alk. paper) — ISBN 0-07-180472-2 (alk. paper)
   1. Employees—Rating of.   2. Performance standards.   I. Russell, Linda. II. Title.
   HF5549.5.R3R8697 2012
   658.3'125—dc23   2012039724

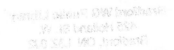

CONTENTS

CONTENTS

Preface

L et's be honest, performance reviews have a bad reputation—for a good reason. They often aren't structured in ways that bring out the best conversation between managers and employees. Instead, managers and employees often approach the annual review with uncertainty, anxiety, and dread. Without a good framework for the review and without the right mindset, tools, or training in how to navigate this sometimes difficult terrain, managers tend to put off reviews until the last minute and employees tend to assume a defensive posture as they steel themselves for their manager's summary judgment of an entire year's worth of effort. Because of these factors, the traditional review as too many of us experience it can be intimidating and fear inducing. It doesn't have to be this way.

We think that it's time to approach performance reviews in a fresh way. Instead of the often one-way managerially driven process of the classical approach, we'd like to propose a more transformational performance coaching conversation. In this approach, the employee actually takes the lead in the process, and the manager, acting as a coach, provides a more facilitative role in guiding the conversation toward insight and learning by both parties. We think that such a coaching conversation is capable of strengthening the performance partnership between the supervisor and employee and moving every employee to star-performer status. When used with the right mindset and a complementary suite of tools and strategies within the larger context of the *great performance management cycle*, the traditional performance review can be reframed into a powerful process that changes the very nature of the performance partnership and builds greater employee ownership of performance results.

There are dozens of books available to you on performance reviews. You can find books that present performance review forms, step-by-step strategies for giving feedback, and tools for diagnosing performance problems. There are phrase books that suggest helpful words and phrases to use when setting goals and giving an employee constructive feedback. Many of these books should be on your bookshelf and within reach as you prepare for an employee's performance review. Each of these books holds a part of the solution needed to build your performance management skill set, but these resources will be most helpful to you when they are used within an overarching, comprehensive, and integrated approach to performance management. Using specific performance review tools, skills, and techniques or conducting performance coaching conversations without fully understanding this larger performance management framework and mindset is like filling your car's gas tank, changing its oil, checking the air pressure in its tires, and driving down the highway without a clear destination or map to guide you. And during your aimless journey you neglect to check the speedometer, oil temperature, and gas gauges as you wander about, hoping that you'll arrive at the right place—wherever that is! It is no wonder why the performance review process can be frustrating!

We think that you'll find that *Fearless Performance Reviews* is quite different from other books on performance management and performance reviews. It presents an innovative approach to performance reviews—which we have renamed performance coaching conversations—that anchors the conversation within the framework of the great performance management cycle. In addition, we offer a powerful new way of thinking about performance management and the performance partnership between managers and their direct reports. Our approach is framed by what we call the *collaborative mindset*—an idea that has the power to profoundly transform how you interact with others, how you manage performance, and how you conduct the performance review. We are confident that this mindset is the strongest possible foundation for conducting coaching conversations, significantly reducing anxiety and fear in both the employee and the manager that often accompanies a more traditional review. We wrote this book to help reduce this fear and to enable managers, through the great performance management cycle and the coaching conversation, to bring out the best performance in everyone. It may be that not every member of your team is capable of becoming a star performer. We believe, however, that as a result of using our approach, which involves embracing the collaborative mindset, the performance coaching conversation, and the related tools that we introduce in *Fearless Performance Reviews*, you will be able to help all of your employees—even those whose performance is mediocre—significantly improve their performance. We deeply believe that when the right mindset, tools, and conditions are in place performance transformation is possible.

Our journey of discovery to find a better approach for performance reviews actually began because of our own personal failures and frustrations with giving and receiving performance feedback. Both of us had searing negative experiences with performance reviews that left permanent scars and had a profound influence upon the way we approach performance management and performance reviews today. *Fearless Performance Reviews* is a culmination of our hard work to find a better way. It also benefits from our years as consultants to a diverse clientele—many of whom have struggled with implementing effective performance management and review systems. Our clients have field tested our models and tools, and our ideas have been further tested and refined in our performance coaching and performance management workshops presented to hundreds of managers and employees over the years.

While we think that we offer you a transformational and comprehensive approach to performance reviews in this book, we don't present you with a "turnkey" performance management system. We don't provide you with model performance review forms and don't recommend a performance rating scale. One of the objectives of this book is to offer an approach to performance management and performance reviews that can be used with any performance management system, and we believe that the models and tools we introduce within these pages meet this objective. At the same time, we also hope that readers will reflect upon our approach to performance management and performance coaching conversations and then take steps to refine, adjust, or redefine their own systems to reflect the ideas embedded within this book.

Because the work you see in *Fearless Performance Reviews* has evolved from our consulting practice and skill-building workshops, we want to thank our many clients who have helped us learn what works and what doesn't. Their collective frustrations with traditional performance review practices and enthusiasm for a new approach kept us active in the search for effective models and approaches to help them find a better way.

We owe special thanks to Donya Dickerson, senior editor at McGraw-Hill. Donya recognized the potential value of this book to the field of performance management, and she encouraged us to translate our innovative ideas, tools, approach, and practices into these pages. We greatly appreciate her vision for bringing this book to life and for her confidence in our abilities to make that happen. We also appreciate the work of Richard Rothschild and his team of editors who worked along with Donya to help bring focus and clarity to our ideas. The ideas within this book benefited from their collective insights on how best to express them.

Our final thanks go to Dr. Chris Argyris for freely granting us permission to use his work and integrate it into our practice and writing. Dr. Argyris's research and writings have had a profound influence on our thinking and especially upon our approach to performance reviews. His theories about defensive strategies and how they undermine healthy dialogue directly inform the models and tools we have developed and use in our consulting, workshops, and books. *Fearless Performance Reviews* wouldn't have been possible without his contributions. Our thinking radically changed when we were first exposed to his work over twenty-five years ago and he continues to inspire us every day.

We hope that this book gives you a personal jump-start toward a more effective approach to conducting your own truly fearless performance reviews. If *Fearless Performance Reviews* moves you closer to that outcome, then we will have accomplished our key goals in writing this book: conducting performance coaching conversations that eliminate fear, strengthen the partnership for performance between you and those who report to you, and enable employees to achieve great performance outcomes.

We'd like to hear from you as you learn and apply the ideas, models, and tools introduced in *Fearless Performance Reviews*. Tell us what you found helpful, even transformational, and let us know too about the things that didn't work for you. We welcome your ideas, suggestions, and questions. It would be great to have an ongoing dialogue with our readers on strategies for creating truly fearless performance coaching conversations. We look forward to hearing from you.

Linda and Jeffrey Russell
RCI@RussellConsultingInc.com
www.RussellConsultingInc.com
Madison, Wisconsin

INTRODUCTION: THE IDEA OF FEARLESS REVIEWS

You know why you've bought this book. Let's be honest—whether you're on the giving or receiving end, if you're like most people, the annual performance review isn't something that you generally look forward to. For better or for worse, you're in good company. For a variety of reasons that we'll explore in this book, the performance review is for many of us an uncomfortable conversation that we would much prefer not to have. Too often the performance review is filled with anxiety and uncertainty and produces results that satisfy no one. But it doesn't have to be this way. We have the choice and opportunity to transform these frequently tense and fear-laden discussions into fearless and productive conversations that help guide an employee toward great performance outcomes while at the same time strengthening the performance partnership between the supervisor and the employee.

Getting your performance reviews to become truly fearless is surprisingly easy, but it requires a fresh perspective and a disciplined approach. The first step of this approach involves adopting a new mindset that opens up the relationship between the supervisor and the employee to enable honest and direct communication. The second step requires seeing the performance review as part of a larger performance management infrastructure that includes goal setting, organizational actions to support performance, and frequent interactions between supervisor and employee. The third step includes doing your homework, which involves exploring the root causes of successes and setbacks, before having the face-to-face performance review. And the fourth and final step involves adopting a new roadmap for conducting the performance review—what we call the *performance coaching conversation*.

What Got Us Here

Performance reviews are a relatively recent phenomenon in the life of organizations. Their roots lie in the early 1900s and the work of Fredrick Taylor with his focus on scientific management, which included the division of responsibilities between managers (thinkers) and employees (doers), standardization of methods based upon scientific research, active training of employees in how to perform their work, and the provision of detailed instructions to all employees in performing their work.

Taylor's work encouraged organizations to guide and manage performance by using a structured and systematic process—all driven by management. Taylor believed that workers didn't have the knowledge to effectively decide how to do their work and that it was up to management to develop detailed plans for defining a job and for deciding how a job was to be done. Once defined by management, job expectations and methods were then to be communicated to the workers.

Whether we agree or disagree with Taylor's rather top-down approach, he had a profound impact on how organizations structured themselves and operated in the early twentieth century. Taylor's theories and methods played an especially prominent role during World War II in how industrial organizations managed their operations and workforce. And it was during this period that the traditional performance review was born as a managerial vehicle for defining performance expectations and for holding workers accountable to these expectations.

So the performance review legacy that we inherit today is steeped in an early twentieth century, top-down, one-way, manager-knows-best tradition that, unfortunately, is not a good fit to our twenty-first century sensibilities that involve an awareness of the importance of employee engagement, the power of employee job ownership, and the value of employee participation in designing and managing their own work. This traditional approach is not aligned with the way that most organizations need to operate today to be sustainably competitive in a global marketplace: dynamic, responsive, and always learning—characteristics that need to be demonstrated at every level in an organization, not just among an elite group of all-knowing managers.

It is imperative that we as individual managers or employees—along with our entire organizations—make a rapid transition away from this inherited approach to performance management (and the reviews that are part of this approach) toward a more appropriate model that embraces employee ownership of the process with individual and organizational learning at the core. If we don't make this transition, we will remain stuck in a Tayloresque world that is ruled by "all-knowing" managers who simply can't know it all. And what are the consequences of this? We will not be able to learn or improve fast enough to stay competitive, and we will lose the energy, creativity, commitment, and ideas of our great employees, who might just go elsewhere to feel heard and engaged. This doesn't seem like a winning and sustainable approach to performance management or to managing an organization in general.

What's called for is a new framework for performance management that turns Taylor's manager-knows-all approach that tends to create divisions and induce fear between managers and their employees into more of a partnership between managers and employees that is focused on learning and growth. And when we achieve this performance partnership, the division and fear dissipates and we are able to conduct truly fearless performance reviews.

What Is a Fearless Performance Review?

Fear is defined as "an unpleasant emotion caused by the threat of danger, pain, or harm."[1] Whether this threat is real or imagined, as long as someone perceives the possibility of danger, pain, or harm, fear is likely to be present. Some synonyms for fear include dread, panic, alarm, bother, worry, fret, stress, and terror. From this definition and the related synonyms, it's clear that when fear is present during a performance review, little learning will take place.

Fearless is defined as "showing a lack of fear,"[2] which translates into a lack of dread, panic, worry, or fret. Synonyms for fearless include bold, courageous, dauntless, brave, gutsy, and valiant. When we are fearless in a given situation, we are bold and courageous as we face the perhaps difficult realities of the situation.

So what is a fearless performance review? A fearless review is an interaction between a supervisor and employee that is characterized by the absence of dread, panic, and worry as well as the presence of courageous and gutsy directness where both parties speak with integrity. Within a fearless review there is open and honest two-way communication where both parties are comfortable speaking and hearing the truth. When engaged in a fearless dialogue about performance issues, both the manager and the employee are focused on insight and learning and no topic is off limits.

During a fearless review, we end up learning as much if not more than the person with whom we're talking. We listen without judging and can speak without feeling judged. We have compassion toward the other person—especially when he irritates us. And we take ownership for our contribution to whatever performance challenge or opportunity the two of us are exploring. All of this, in turn, enables us to mutually explore the causes of performance challenges and roadblocks and find new ways of working together that overcome these challenges and move us both toward achieving our common goals.

Consider the profound implications for fearless reviews: How would it change things if you were able to structure your performance reviews to be truly fearless? What would it feel like to approach your reviews with a sense of excitement and possibility for guiding others toward great performance outcomes?

While the idea of fearless reviews sounds great, in reality they can be kind of scary: speaking authentically, no sugarcoating the truth, cutting to the heart of an issue, being honest in asking someone to change, and taking responsibility for our own part in performance failures. While we value these things and recognize that we can't become a great manager or achieve great performance without such honesty and ownership, we also might feel anxious because we're not sure where to start or how to forge this kind of relationship with others.

Let's Get Started!

Fearless Performance Reviews lays out a practical framework and road-map that helps address any anxieties you may have about moving in this direction. You will discover that once you adopt a transformational way of thinking called the collaborative mindset, all the necessary components begin to fall into place to support fearless performance conversations. The models and tools that we share with you can be used on their own to facilitate more effective reviews or they can be used in conjunction with your organization's existing performance management system (e.g., expectations, forms, methodologies, and policies). You won't need to reinvent your organization's performance management system—only your mental models about performance management, your view of those whom you are reviewing, and your role within the entire performance management and review process.

In Chapters 1 through 4 we'll examine the problems with the traditional approach to performance reviews, highlight the counterproductive *my-way mindset* that too often informs the entire process, and dig deeper into why this undermining mindset and the traditional review tend to induce fear in both managers and employees.

Chapters 5 through 9 introduce the transformational *collaborative mindset* as a powerful way for reframing how both managers and employees view their partnership and how they constructively engage each other around performance management and performance reviews. In these chapters you will discover how to find the courage, boldness, and audacity to speak honestly and directly to others.

Conducting fearless reviews depends, of course, upon a clear understanding of the purposes of the performance review. We'll review these purposes in Chapter 10 and discuss the importance of shifting away from the traditional review to one that's based upon the collaborative mindset and is more likely to reduce fear within the process.

In Chapter 11 we position performance reviews within a larger performance management infrastructure called the great performance management cycle. This foundational cycle offers an integrated approach to performance management that sets the stage for every performance review to guide an employee toward achieving great performance outcomes.

Understanding and diagnosing the root causes of great performance as well as when things go wrong is the focus for Chapter 12. In this chapter you'll learn about the most common drivers of performance success and some strategies for exploring the origins of performance challenges. The insights from this chapter will help you prepare for the performance review and help move more of your employees to star-performer status.

Informed by the collaborative mindset within the great performance management cycle and by an understanding of the root causes of performance successes and problems, your next step is to begin preparing for the face-to-face review. Chapter 13, Laying a Foundation for Success, offers methods and strategies to help you prepare for conducting a fearless review. In this chapter you'll develop your plan for the review and gain confidence in your ability to navigate through the surprises and sometimes-rocky emotions that come up during the review.

Chapters 14 through 16 introduce a simple yet transformational pathway for conducting the performance review. You will learn how our simple performance coaching conversation model integrates the collaborative mindset and the other tools introduced in the book into a powerful framework for conducting the coaching conversation instead of a fear-inducing review. When you integrate the methodology of the performance coaching conversation into your approach to performance reviews, the two-way dialogue helps dissipate fear (in both of you) and strengthens insight, learning, and growth toward the larger purpose of enabling employees to achieve great results. At the end of the day, that's what counts, and by the time you're done reading this book you'll have the confidence and the ability to make that happen.

We'll guide you along this journey to fearless reviews by sharing what works and helping you to avoid what doesn't. We'll share tools and best practices that will help you conduct meaningful performance reviews that are free of fear. And once you master the collaborative mindset, you'll come to realize that this new mental model alone is likely to transform not only your performance reviews but all of your personal and professional relationships as well. We're excited about that possibility, and we hope that you are too!

Let's begin the journey into fearless reviews!

FEARLESS
PERFORMANCE
REVIEWS

WHY THE FEAR IN REVIEWS?

> *If people are good only because they fear punishment, and hope*
> *for reward, then we are a sorry lot indeed.*
>   —Albert Einstein, German-born theoretical physicist

Years ago, our client Brenda called us because she was afraid. Her performance review was coming up the next week, and she was concerned about being ambushed and blindsided by her manager. "I know this guy all too well," she said, "and I just don't trust him." Brenda went on to ask if we would be willing to sit in on the review to keep things accurate and, more importantly, safe.

Our response to Brenda was cautious: "That's not a role that we typically play," we said, "but we're open to the possibility. Let us think about this a bit and get back to you." We were somewhat hesitant because we normally don't get involved in facilitating supervisor–employee discussions.

About 30 minutes later, while we were still pondering whether to get involved, our phone rang again. This time it was a supervisor on the line, saying that he had a performance review with a difficult employee the following week. "I was wondering," Tom asked, "if you'd be willing to sit in on this review to keep things more level headed. Frankly, this employee is pretty volatile, and I'd like someone there as an insurance policy. I find her pretty intimidating, and," he added, "I just don't trust her."

Yes, you guessed it. Tom was Brenda's supervisor. Without hesitating, we said yes to Tom's request—with the qualifier, "as long as Brenda's open to us being there." Tom clearly sounded relieved. Tom said that he'd clear it with Brenda and that, unless we heard from him to the contrary, he would see us at the review the following week.

What Brings Out the Fear?

So why did Tom and Brenda feel anxiety and fear as they each approached this annual performance review? What caused them to dread this encounter so much that they needed a third party to mediate what should have been a pretty straightforward discussion of the past year of Brenda's performance?

Before we get into the origins of fear in Brenda and Tom's situation, let's step back from their unique relationship and explore what it is about performance reviews in general that too often brings anxiety, if not fear, bubbling to the surface in both employees and supervisors.

In our experience, performance reviews often produce uncomfortable feelings in both parties due to the following reasons.

It Seems There's a Lot at Stake

And sometimes there is! Organizations often try to pack a lot into performance reviews—expecting them to be a primary driver of merit-based raises, anchoring promotions to good reviews, surfacing high potentials based upon review ratings, and so forth. Beyond the stakes set by the organization, there are even higher stakes from both the employee's and supervisor's perspectives.

For employees the personal and professional stakes include professional competence, credibility, and reputation; self-esteem and self-worth; job security; career growth and opportunities; and personal pride. These stakes are unique in that they aren't defined by organizations but by employees themselves. A sense of self-worth and professional integrity as well as possible career growth contribute to the importance and potential long-term consequences of the performance review.

But what's at stake for supervisors? Aren't they just raising the stakes for employees? What do they have on the line? For anyone who has held the title of supervisor, the stakes at performance reviews are just as clear as they are for employees: a sense of competence as a supervisor, the ability to maintain a sense of control or influence over the situation, the feeling of responsibility for employees' performance failures, and future career growth as a manager or leader at the organization.

The Process Seems Overly Judgmental

For employees, the anxiety and fear arise in part from the perception that their professional accomplishments and contributions are being judged as worthy or not. Rather than a forward-leaning developmental method, the performance review has a reputation as a backward-looking process that examines an entire year's worth of the employee's performance and then grades that performance as exemplary, good, satisfactory, needing improvement, or unacceptable. Employees feel judged when their entire performance life seems to have been reduced to a checkbox. And why shouldn't they feel anxiety and even fear about that?

Not surprisingly, supervisors have as much difficulty with passing judgment as employees have with being judged. They may not feel confident that they know the employee's work well enough to accurately assess the employee's performance. Even if supervisors feel comfortable with the accuracy of a performance assessment, they may still feel uncomfortable knowing that their judgment of an employee's performance is likely to have an impact upon the employee's image, reputation, and future success at the organization. Checking a box on the performance review form seems easy to do, but good supervisors understand the impact of such judgments. And that's a heavy—and frightening—burden to have on their shoulders.

The Review Process Sometimes Raises Uncomfortable Truths

The greatest value of a performance review comes from an honest discussion of what's working and what's not. Unfortunately, for many people, getting to that level of honesty is hard. It's hard to hear it, and it's hard to speak it.

Who wants to hear their boss point out mistakes they have made? Who enjoys hearing their supervisor talk about an oversight or a bad decision that led to less-than-desirable outcomes? Yes, "to err is human," but none of us wants to make mistakes or be exposed by others as someone who is flawed.

How does it feel for the person sharing these truths? Speaking truthfully can be pretty uncomfortable. Supervisors often don't have the communication skill set to speak clearly and directly about employees' performance shortcomings and failures. Not having the skills or the self-confidence to share these uncomfortable truths raises the supervisor's anxiety level even further. What's the best way to deal with the employee's reaction to constructive feedback? What's the most effective strategy to use when the employee becomes defensive, denies that there's a problem, cries, or blames others? It can be difficult to handle these situations tactfully.

People May Feel Blamed for a Problem

Due to many of the aforementioned sources of fear in performance reviews and because the review is focused on the employee's performance, there is a tendency for the employee being reviewed to feel blamed for performance problems rather than to use the review to examine underlying causes of performance challenges. And, unfortunately, blame never really moves any performance conversation toward a positive outcome. While it might get someone's attention, blame usually just results in defensiveness and denial. When people feel blamed they tend to go undercover.

4

People Aren't Skilled at Performance Reviews

It's actually quite rare for someone to sit us down and teach us how to either give or receive feedback gracefully or effectively. When training supervisors in the performance review process, too much time is spent on how to fill out the review form and too little time on how to structure the conversation. At best the skills training for supervisors covers such topics as how to give constructive feedback (e.g., focus on behaviors not the person, make it timely, be descriptive), and at worst supervisors are introduced to the infamous "sandwich" technique: start with what the employee is doing well, shift to where the employee needs improvement, and then end with another positive affirmation about the employee's performance. A further complicating factor is that we don't do them often enough to refine the skills we do have. The once-a-year review doesn't facilitate our ability to learn what works and what doesn't. On the whole, the lack of useful training and the infrequency of reviews lead to supervisors not having the skills they need to make the review a meaningful, two-way dialogue about the employee's performance.

Oddly, organizations expend almost no effort at building employees' skills in receiving feedback or playing a proactive and leading role during the performance review. Too often employees are seen as passive receivers of the review rather than active and equal contributors. As a result, without supervisors having the right skills or mindset to facilitate constructive engagement and learning, uncertainty, anxiety, and fear tend to loom large in an employee's mind leading up to and during the review.

There's Too Much Uncertainty

Reviews are often filled with surprises that catch both the employee and supervisor off guard. If reviews occur only once or twice a year or if the relationship between the players is strained, this is even more likely to occur. In the absence of frequent and ongoing performance conversations throughout the year, neither party to the review knows what to expect.

From the supervisor's perspective, uncertainty comes in the form of not knowing how the employee will react to performance feedback or not knowing what information the employee has about performance challenges that, once shared, might compel the supervisor to reassess her understanding of the causes and solutions to such challenges.

From an employee's perspective, uncertainty comes from not knowing what performance issues the supervisor will raise during the review. Will the supervisor focus on problems or challenges from the distant past? Will she focus on recent issues where the employee may have struggled? Will the supervisor share feedback from peers, clients, customers, or other departments regarding the employee's past performance? With uncertainty about what issues will be raised during the review, employees are likely to be anxious and fearful.

People Feel a Loss of Control

Performance reviews often create situations (due to the issues cited above) where one or both parties to the review feel that their ability to maintain control over their work life or future is likely to be impaired. Due to the fact that the supervisor, in the end, gets to determine the final performance assessment along with the consequences of this assessment on the employee's salary, career potential, status in the organization, and so forth, an employee may feel powerless to effectively influence this final assessment—especially if the relationship between the two of them isn't strong.

Supervisors might also feel a loss of control during a performance review because they may not be able to control the direction of the conversation. As you will learn in Chapter 2, we believe that control is an illusion. A supervisor focused on maintaining control during a performance review is taking precisely the wrong approach. If the supervisor is attempting to control the review conversation to ensure that the employee agrees with the review rating and accepts the next steps for improving performance going forward, the supervisor will likely experience anxiety and fear that something during the review is likely to go wrong.

Many Performance Reviews Tend to Be One-Way Conversations

The annual review tends to be one-sided: the supervisor presents an overview of his assessment of the employee's past year of performance, and the employee listens and responds. While sometimes supervisors take steps to make the process more interactive, because supervisors usually drive the performance review conversation, the employee's involvement in the process tends to be more reactive than interactive.

This one-way conversation creates anxiety for the supervisor who feels responsible for doing most of the heavy lifting: doing a performance analysis, identifying the employee's strengths and improvement areas, examining the causes of performance problems, identifying goals for the review, and anticipating and preparing for the employee's reactions. Carrying the weight of leading this process while at the same time being fair and doing the right thing for the employee creates a lot of stress and anxiety—not to mention eats up a lot of time.

The one-sided nature of this process also creates anxiety for the employee for obvious reasons: the employee is in a reactive and/ or defensive mode, the supervisor sets the agenda for the discussion and may focus on a narrow set of performance outcomes rather than maintaining a balanced and holistic perspective, and finally— because the employee is reacting to the supervisor's assessment—he may not feel comfortable asserting a narrative that is different from the supervisor's.

In any given performance review only some of these anxiety- or fear-inducing characteristics may be in effect for one or both parties. In other cases, all of them can come into play in ways that make a meaningful process almost impossible to achieve.

Let's return to the performance review example that we started this chapter with: Brenda and Tom. The sources of Brenda's fear and

7

anxiety as the review approached emerged from a confluence of the causes that we've listed above:

- There was a lot at stake for her—particularly her sense of self-esteem and competence as well as her reputation and image within the company.
- She believed that she was being unfairly judged and would be labeled as less than a star performer.
- She was sure that Tom would bring up performance problems in a way that would make her feel like a failure.
- She thought that she would be blamed for things that were outside her control.
- She wasn't sure what would be included in Tom's feedback to her (uncertainty).
- She felt that Tom was in the driver's seat and that she was locked in the trunk. She felt powerless to offer what she believed would be a more accurate assessment of her performance.
- Based upon her past experience with Tom's approach to reviews, she knew that it would be a one-way review with little opportunity for her to tell a different story—except by reacting defensively on issues that she expected him to raise during the review.

Brenda essentially feared the review because she believed that Tom was biased against her and had already judged her performance as a problem.

So that's what was going through Brenda's head prior to the review. But, what were the likely causes of supervisor Tom's fear and anxiety as the day approached?

Like Brenda, he too felt that there was a lot at stake—his credibility and competence as a supervisor were on the line, and, from his perspective, he seemed to be losing control of the situation to the extent that he didn't believe he could manage the review effectively, especially considering what he saw as Brenda's stubbornness. Tom was also fearful of raising uncomfortable truths—his perceptions of Brenda's performance problems—knowing that she would push back hard.

There's more. To put it simply, Tom just didn't know how to conduct the review. Although he had been a supervisor for years, he never felt comfortable structuring and navigating the process. This was especially true whenever he was dealing with an employee, like Brenda, who he felt was having performance problems. Finally, Tom was anxious and fearful of the review with Brenda because he felt that it was up to him to drive the conversation—that it was his job to lead the process and give her feedback. And he didn't expect to get much help from Brenda. If anything, he expected her to be defensive and argumentative. For Tom this wasn't going to be easy, and that's why he sought out our assistance to help keep things as pleasant as possible, given the circumstances, and to ensure that Brenda heard what she needed to hear and then agreed to take the right actions to improve her performance in the proceeding year.

So, just imagine what this coming together looked like: two people, uncomfortable with honest conversation, fearful of the process, and mistrusting the motives and intentions of each other, trying to have a meaningful discussion about Brenda's job performance over the past 12 months. Even with us acting as a neutral third party to ensure a civil discourse, this performance review was not likely to go well.

THE MY-WAY MINDSET

In Part 1 of *Fearless Performance Reviews* we describe a powerful mindset that helps create a significant amount of anxiety for both supervisors and employees. In Chapter 2 we share the foundations of the my-way mindset and explain why people engage in behaviors that lead them away from insight, learning, and genuine performance improvement.

Chapter 3 examines the governing values and underlying assumptions of this counterproductive mindset and gives examples of how these values and assumptions undermine the effectiveness of performance reviews. And in Chapter 4 we complete our review of the my-way mindset by exploring the enacting behaviors that result from these values and assumptions and move both supervisor and employee further from a productive performance conversation.

It should be obvious by the end of Part 1 that our goal is to steer you away from the my-way mindset as an operating system for creating fearless reviews. While our recommended mindset is discussed in Part 2, we think it is important to first establish how the my-way mindset works in order to ensure that you avoid this fear-inducing approach.

2

WHAT IS THE MY-WAY MINDSET?

> *Freedom is good . . . but control is better.*
> —Vladimir Ilyich Lenin

When looking at our long list of factors that contribute fear and anxiety to reviews, the fix seems rather simple—just do the opposite: reduce the stakes, lose the judgment, don't raise uncomfortable truths (a strategy which, of course, isn't very helpful in the short or long run), lose the blame, develop skills at giving and receiving performance feedback, reduce the uncertainty, give up the need to control, and make the conversation truly two-way. While many of these steps could indeed improve the quality of most performance reviews (with the one notable exception being ignoring uncomfortable truths), correcting just these simple sources of fear and anxiety, we believe, won't be sufficient to make the review a meaningful conversation.

There is something much deeper that drives all of the fear-inducing factors that we have cited in this chapter: the larger mindset that both the supervisor and the employee unconsciously adopt as a framework for how they see themselves and the other party in this performance relationship.

What is a mindset, and why does it matter? Merriam-Webster's dictionary defines *mindset* as "a mental attitude or inclination; a fixed state of mind." In our view, a mindset is a mental model or way of thinking and seeing that people often unconsciously adopt that influences how they interpret and respond to others and the world. A mindset is a relatively fixed mental attitude or disposition that predetermines an individual's interpretations of and responses to different situations. Mindset matters because, within the partnership between the supervisor and employee (and especially during performance reviews), each person's mindset contributes to the quality of the connection. The most useful mindset will cultivate a positive relationship and lead to a meaningful review. A less-than-optimal mindset can lead to a relationship and review that are defined by anxiety and fear.

Figure 2.1 displays what we believe is the single most important mindset continuum influencing the strength of the partnership for performance and the meaningfulness of the performance review: the *my-way–collaborative mindset continuum.*

As you can see, the my-way end of the continuum is broadly characterized as seeing the world in rather black-and-white terms, whereas the collaborative end of the continuum is very much the opposite. In any situation, individuals make a decision (consciously or unconsciously) as to where they will fall along this continuum. Many people have a natural set point along this continuum—some naturally embrace the collaborative mindset as their approach to life, while others lean toward the my-way mindset. This set point deeply influences the overall quality of a person's relationships and life in general.

My-Way Mindset	◄ - - - - - - - - - - ►	Collaborative Mindset
I am right; you are wrong. I'm in charge; you're not. My version of the truth is the right one. I need to win; you need to lose.	In every situation and in every relationship you choose a position on this mindset continuum.	I have something to learn. People are doing their best. I only know part of the story. We both can win.

FIGURE 2.1 The My-Way Mindset–Collaborative Mindset Conntinuum

Above and beyond their natural inclination, however, for each specific relationship and in every situation, people consciously or unconsciously choose a position along this mindset continuum. And the choice they make in a given relationship or situation ultimately determines the quality of the relationship and their response to the situation. This is especially true for the relationship between a supervisor and an employee—the quality of their interactions, the effectiveness of their communication, and the overall effectiveness of the performance review.

Unfortunately, research suggests that in stressful situations—in circumstances where people are surprised, judged, second guessed, or feeling uneasy or uncomfortable—people tend to move toward the my-way end of the continuum. The my-way mindset enables those who embrace it to feel as if they can maintain control in the situation, escape blame for failures or mistakes, dodge the bullet of responsibility and accountability, and avoid a personal or professional embarrassment.

Chris Argyris and Donald Schön, in their groundbreaking book *Theory in Practice*, and Argyris in his follow-up work *Knowledge for Action*, offer some useful insights into why people use the my-way mindset and how they enact it. Argyris and Schön suggest that each of us has two theories of action inside our heads that we routinely call upon when we are presented with situations that require a response: our *espoused theory* (i.e., what we say we will do in a situation) and our *theory-in-use* (i.e., what we actually do in the situation). Argyris and Schön argue that the problem with our theory-in-use is that it almost always operates below our radar; we are unaware that it is steering our behaviors and actions, even while we may espouse the opposite. Nonetheless, there it is, nudging us to act in ways that actually run counter to what we say we believe and intend to do. An example of this is when we say we value another person's opinion or ideas, yet when this person shares a perspective that is contrary to our own thinking we act in ways that are dismissive and discounting of the other person's viewpoint or idea.

This disconnection between what we say and what we actually do is especially prevalent when we find ourselves in difficult, stressful, or uncomfortable situations in which we feel threatened, exposed, or vulnerable. When we are embarrassed or psychologically threatened, we tend to activate a theory-in-use that, unfortunately, leads us into defensiveness, denial, blame, rationalization, and justification. This, in turn, leads to higher levels of misunderstanding and conflict with others. The deteriorating relationships that result further impair our ability to make the right decisions and do the right thing. As if this wasn't bad enough, our actions are worsened by the fact that most of this is occurring outside of our conscious awareness. The net effect is significant erosion of our personal effectiveness and continuing deterioration of our relationships with those who are involved in the situation. Unfortunately, in their research Argyris and Schön found that this theory-in-use is the default strategy people tend to adopt as a way to save face, escape exposure to vulnerability in situations, and maintain a sense of control in circumstances in which they feel challenged, threatened, embarrassed, and so forth.

This counterproductive approach is called the Model 1 theory-in-use by Argyris and Schön. Putnam, Smith, and McArthur at Action Design renamed this theory-in-use the unilateral control model, which is also the term used by Roger Schwarz in his book *The Skilled Facilitator* (2002). Building upon these earlier efforts, we have integrated the key elements from these action science models and the work of William Isaacs on facilitating dialogue (*Dialogue,* 1999) and Susan Scott (*Fierce Conversations,* 2004), merged them with insights from our own practice as consultants, and renamed this theory-in-use the my-way mindset. The my-way mindset is characterized by defensive reasoning, a desire to win rather than lose, and an absence of insight and learning. When our mindset is focused on my-way unilateralism, we are predisposed to a relatively narrow range of interpretations of and responses to various situations. This is especially true when our mindset flies below our radar, or our conscious awareness.

Figure 2.2 displays the my-way mindset as it functions at the extreme left-hand side of the mindset continuum displayed in Figure 2.1. As you'll see when we explore this mindset in greater detail, the values, assumptions, and enacting behaviors of this unilateral approach often drive our thinking and behaviors in a direction that moves us away from insight and learning.

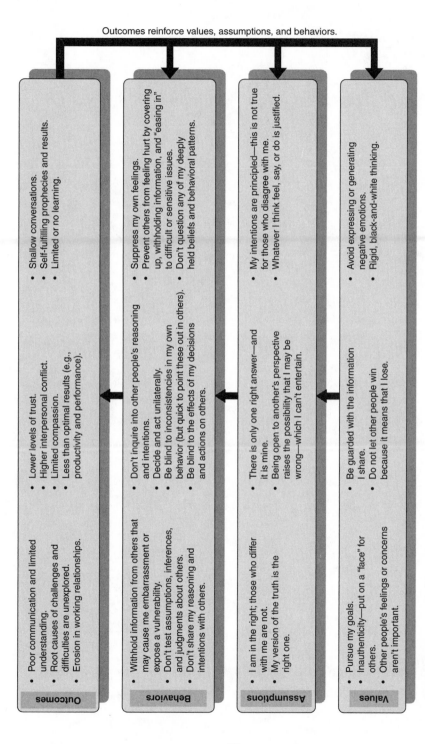

FIGURE 2.2 The My-Way Mindset

Source: Adapted from the work of Chris Argyris, Donald Schön, Action Design, Roger Schwarz, William Isaacs, and Susan Scott

17

CHAPTER

3

GOVERNING VALUES AND UNDERLYING ASSUMPTIONS OF THE MY-WAY MINDSET

> *An eye for an eye and we all will be blind.*
> —Mahatma Gandhi, Indian statesman and nationalist

When we are faced with a stressful, embarrassing, or psychologically threatening situation—such as a performance review—our my-way mindset tends to push aside our collaborative approach in order to reduce the stress, avoid the embarrassment, and escape the threat. As noted in Figure 2.2, this mindset includes a set of governing values, assumptions, and enacting behaviors that, taken together, protect the individual from uncomfortable information and allow the person to maintain the illusion of control.

Let's first take a closer look at the governing values of the my-way mindset to examine how these values—which serve as the foundation of this mindset—might shape a person's worldview and how they are likely to influence the assumptions, behaviors, and finally the outcomes within a performance management relationship and the performance review itself.

Pursue My Goals

This governing value involves an overriding commitment by the person to pursue his agenda—and to do whatever it takes to realize these goals. In a performance review this governing value might mean a supervisor aggressively pursues a strategy to get an employee to accept full responsibility for a performance problem. For an employee this value might involve a strong defense of his self-worth by shifting responsibility for a performance problem to someone else.

Inauthenticity—Put on a Face for Others

While we rarely acknowledge a desire to be inauthentic—to speak or act in ways that are contrary to our inner thoughts—being inauthentic enables us to maintain some control over how others perceive us. In the interest of protecting the self, this governing value drives someone to present a "face" to others that she wants others to see but which doesn't reflect her true underlying beliefs, feelings, or thoughts. In a performance review a supervisor might be inauthentic when putting on a face that says, "I really want to hear what you have to say," while thinking to himself, "This whole process is a waste of time. She isn't interested in being a contributing member of this team."

An employee holding this value during a review might give the impression that she agrees with the supervisor while thinking, "I'll just agree in order to get this conversation over with—and then do what I had planned to do anyway."

Other People's Feelings or Concerns Aren't Important

This governing value reflects a focus on self-interest versus understanding and responding to the needs of others. When people feel exposed, vulnerable, threatened, or embarrassed, this value basically says to take care of themselves first and ignore others' needs. You come first, others don't count—at least while you are defending yourself.

During a performance review a supervisor might reflect this value by thinking, "My concerns about the employee's performance are the most important thing here. I am less interested in what she thinks or what she feels. My needs come first." An employee might be driven by a similar belief: "This is all about my supervisor hearing my voice, my issues, and my concerns. My needs come first in this situation."

Be Guarded with the Information that I Share

Information gives people power. If people have a lot of information about us, they might use that information in ways that gives them more power over us than we would like them to have. As such, this governing value encourages unilateralists to hold back information that could be used by others in ways that might frustrate their goals.

Related to this, unilateralists believe that they can maintain greater control over situations when others know only what the unilateralists want them to know. During a performance review a supervisor might demonstrate this value by not sharing information with the employee that the supervisor might find embarrassing—such as the fact that the supervisor doesn't feel very competent at coaching others or that she lacks the confidence needed to raise performance issues prior to the annual review. An employee might express this value by not sharing information about a recent mistake he has made that no one has discovered—yet.

Do Not Let Other People Win

My-way unilateralists see the world as a zero-sum game where for every winner there has to be a loser. If they see the other side winning, unilateralists believe that they must be losing. Because unilateralists need to win (achieve their goals) and believe that they and the other side cannot both win at the same time, they can't let others win. In a performance review, this value might translate into the supervisor failing to acknowledge that an employee might have a point when she complains that the timeline for achieving a challenging goal was unrealistic. Admitting that the employee is right (letting her win) suggests that the supervisor was perhaps wrong (losing)—something that a my-way unilateralist wouldn't be able to accept. For an employee, this zero-sum value would manifest itself similarly. For example, an employee refuses to accept that his supervisor has a legitimate concern related to recent customer complaints about his performance. Doing so would mean that the supervisor is winning on this issue and that he must be losing.

Avoid Expressing or Generating Negative Emotions

The expression of negative emotions by either party might lead to greater discomfort in both parties, which can distract one or both from their goals, which, in turn, can lead to a loss of control. This value essentially says, "Don't get upset, and don't let others get upset; it will distract you from your goal." Negative emotions introduce uncertainty into every conversation, so the my-way unilateralist will do everything that he can to prevent such volatility. This might involve speaking dishonestly, sugarcoating bad news, telling half-truths, and so forth all in order to get the other party to agree or comply. During a performance review this value might involve the supervisor controlling her frustration with an employee or not bringing up certain topics that are likely to cause the employee to get upset. The supervisor still actively pursues her goal of getting the employee to agree or comply with something but approaches the conversation in a way that prevents emotions from derailing the agenda. Very much like the supervisor in the review, the employee too might resist expressing anger or frustration (even though he might feel it) or stop short of saying things that might cause the supervisor to react negatively—all to achieve the goal of getting through the review in the smallest amount of time or with the shortest list of improvement areas. Unfortunately, by not sharing genuine feelings—even those that might be negative—honesty and a meaningful conversation remain elusive.

Rigid, Black-and-White Thinking

The unilateralist sees the world in very black-and-white terms: I am right; the other person is wrong. I have a complete understanding of the situation; the other person does not. My goals and objectives are aimed toward the greater good of the person, team, and company; the goals of the other person are not. This duality—closely aligned with the zero-sum, win-lose strategy we alluded to earlier—allows the my-way unilateralist to maintain a sense of virtuousness: I am on the good side of things; the other party is not. In the unilateralist's world, there are no shades of gray. In a performance review, a supervisor's black-and-white thinking is easily seen in a mentality and set of behaviors that say, "I know what the problem is here. My employee is just in denial about this. She just doesn't get it." Of course, the employee's rigid, black-and-white thinking can express itself in exactly the same way!

Understanding the governing values of the my-way mindset is crucial if we are to appreciate how a unilateralist sees the world and how this worldview translates into a set of congruent assumptions and enacting behaviors that result in consequences that are counterproductive to the wellbeing of the unilateralist's relationships.

Underlying Assumptions of the My-Way Mindset

The governing values that we've explored directly lead to a set of assumptions about ourselves, others, and the world that naturally flow from the unilateralism of the my-way approach. As highlighted in Figure 2.2, these assumptions include the following.

I Am Right; Those Who Differ with Me Are Not

This assumption directly evolves from the rigid, black-and-white nature of the my-way mindset. In a performance review both parties can let this assumption lead them to a firm belief in the righteousness of his own position.

My Version of the Truth Is the Right One

This is another assumption based upon the unilateralists' my-way belief that she has the right view, while those on the opposing side do not. This assumption is especially troublesome when a supervisor "knows" the solution to a problem and isn't open to hearing an alternative viewpoint.

There Is Only One Right Answer, and It Is Mine

The values of achieving my goals; other people's feelings or concerns aren't important; do not let others win; and rigid, black-and-white thinking all contribute to this assumption. For this assumption, similar to the previous assumption, each party in a performance review settles into a firm mindset that says, "Only I know the solution to this problem or situation."

Being Open to Another Person's Perspective Raises the Possibility That I May Be Wrong

This assumption seals the my-way unilateralists off from other viewpoints or opinions, which, in turn, narrows the range of options and alternatives available to them. Because being right; winning and not losing; being uninterested in other people's feelings or concerns; achieving their goals; and rigid, black-and-white thinking all drive this assumption, it's difficult for unilateralists to hear things that don't already conform to their own way of thinking. During a performance review this assumption prevents both the supervisor and employee from hearing alternative viewpoints, which causes their thinking to get stuck where it was before the performance conversation began.

My Intentions Are Principled; This is Not True for Those Who Disagree with Me

My-way unilateralists use this underlying assumption to reinforce the righteousness of their own goals while dismissing the goals, feelings, and concerns of others as unimportant or just plain wrong. This breeds mistrust and guardedness with information in unilateralists based upon the fear that sharing too much information with the other party might lead to that other party winning or exerting control over them. In a performance review this leads to both the supervisor and employee entering the conversation in a defensive posture that involves each asserting the righteousness of his position while discounting the other's position.

Whatever I Think, Feel, Say, or Do Is Justified

Because my-way unilateralists believe they are right and others are wrong, don't trust the motives or intentions of the other person, and will do almost anything to win and achieve their goals, it follows that they would embrace the assumption that whatever they think, feel, say, or do is fully justifiable. This "end-justifies-the-means" approach is at the root of much of the suffering in the world today—people saying things or taking actions that they justify according to their belief system despite the pain and hardship that such words and actions can create for others. When, during a performance review, the supervisor decides to unilaterally take away some of the employee's autonomy—or when an employee decides to unilaterally ignore the supervisor's request to correct a problem in a specific way—a supposedly justifiable action significantly undermines both the relationship and performance outcomes.

CHAPTER

ENACTING BEHAVIORS OF THE MY-WAY UNILATERALIST

Furious activity is no substitute for understanding.
—H. H. Williams

As we've explored the governing values and underlying assumptions of the my-way mindset, we've shared examples of the ways in which these values and assumptions might translate into specific behaviors during and likely after a fear-inducing performance review.

As displayed in Figure 2.2, there is an array of behaviors that directly reflect the values and assumptions of the my-way mindset.

Withhold Information From Others that May Cause Me Embarrassment or Expose a Vulnerability

During a performance review where one person may not trust the intentions of the other party, why would she share information that the other person could use to undermine her goals? This withholding is a defensive behavior to protect the my-way unilateralist from further embarrassment or the loss of control.

Don't Test Assumptions, Inferences, and Judgments About Others

Someone following the my-way mindset creates a story that explains someone else's behavior but fails to actually test the validity of that story. These assumptions lead to inferential leaps that enable the my-way unilateralist to "predict" likely future behavior. Over time, these assumptions and inferences lead to firm judgments about others that conveniently put people in neat little boxes. Assumptions, inferences, and judgments are used by all of us as an expedient way to quickly decide how we should act around another person. Especially in situations where we may have limited time and information available to us, assumptions, inferences, and judgments enable us to move forward and make decisions. But there is a problem with making assumptions and rushing to judgment: we may be wrong! Everything we've assumed about the other person or the judgment we've formed may be partially or completely divorced from the actual facts of the situation. Unfortunately, my-way unilateralists are often unaware that they have created stories in the first place. When unilateralists make assumptions, inferences, or judgments, they are essentially making final verdicts. For my-way unilateralists, situations are exactly as they understand them—no second thoughts, no doubts or uncertainties.

We've seen this behavior in full force in many performance reviews. Supervisors—if they embrace the my-way mindset—enter reviews with a full suite of assumptions and judgments about their employees. These might include the following: She isn't committed to this project. He is actively undermining me in front of the team. She is unwilling to share information with others. He just doesn't care about this job.

With these assumptions and judgments in place, the unilateralist tends to look for confirming evidence of these assumptions and judgments rather than questioning or setting aside such preconceived notions. Unfortunately, employees following the my-way mindset bring their own set of assumptions, inferences, and judgments about their supervisors. These might include the following: She doesn't believe in my abilities. He has already made up his mind about my potential. She is untrustworthy. He is trying to get rid of me. She has no interest in helping me succeed; this is just about documenting my failures.

It isn't hard to imagine how difficult it would be to have a meaningful performance coaching conversation when both the supervisor and employee embrace the stories that each has created about the other as facts.

Don't Share My Reasoning and Intentions

This enacting behavior involves unilateralists making assertions without feeling the need to explain the reasons or intentions behind the statements. Because unilateralists believe that they are right and that the others are wrong, explanation, argument, and justification are a waste of time. So, instead of explaining one's reasoning and intentions, those who follow the my-way mindset simply make strong declarations and unilaterally try to persuade, impose, or enforce their position without explaining why it makes sense.

We once worked with a unilateralist manager who summed it up nicely: "I don't have to explain myself. I'm the boss, and my employee should just step in line and do what I ask. He doesn't need to know my reasons; he just needs to go along to get along." Obviously, the mindset of this manager led to significant unhappiness among the employees, who rarely understood the reasons behind the manager's decisions and actions.

In a performance review this enacting behavior may lead to one or both parties hearing assertions, declarations, arguments, and positions without understanding the reasons behind the words. And when both parties bring this strategy to the review, the result usually involves arguments over who is right rather than a discussion about the reasoning behind their respective assertions or positions. Both sides stubbornly dig in and defend their positions, further polarizing the relationship and making no progress toward achieving understanding, reconciliation, or resolution. The deeper underlying issues and reasoning behind their respective positions remain unexplored.

Don't Inquire Into Others' Reasoning and Intentions

This enacting behavior closely mirrors the previous behavior. Unilateralists neither share their own reasoning nor have interest in exploring the reasoning and intentions of others—largely because they think that it's a waste of time. Why explore the reasoning or intentions of someone who they think is wrong at best or working against their interests at worst? In a performance review this appears as two people talking at each other without either asking probing questions. And if both the supervisor and employee adopt this approach, as with the previous behavior, the result is positioning and lectures without genuine dialogue or understanding; neither party is interested in understanding the other party's interests, reasoning, or intentions.

Decide and Act Unilaterally

This behavior is a broad and direct reflection of the my-way mindset. Why share decision making if you don't have to? Why invite someone to mutually decide something if you believe that they are fundamentally wrong? Unilateralists adopt this behavior because they can, even when in a subordinate role; they simply take unilateral action without consulting or involving the other party. Supervisors sometimes get lulled into embracing this behavior because others view it as part of their job description. The best managers realize that titles such as manager and supervisor actually get in the way of their effectiveness because others in the organization often expect them to be unilateral when dealing with issues—especially performance issues. So, in performance reviews it's sometimes tempting for supervisors to lean on their title or authority and simply make the decision or take unilateral action when disagreements emerge with an employee.

Following a performance review, employees can decide to act unilaterally by choosing to ignore the suggestions of a supervisor, independently deciding how they will act going forward.

Be Blind to Inconsistencies in My Own Behavior

Because people who enact the my-way mindset believe that they are doing the right thing for the right reasons, all of their behaviors are internally consistent and logically defensible. Their logic goes something like this: Those with whom the my-way unilateralist disagrees are *not* acting with integrity and consistency, and their actions are not logically defensible. And, because others are wrong, untrustworthy, and likely operate from a questionable moral framework, the unilateralist easily finds behaviors in others that demonstrate their inconsistencies. During a performance review either party might be quick to point a finger at how the other person has violated some agreement or understanding while at the same time not seeing how he might be behaving inconsistently.

Be Blind to the Effects of My Decisions and Actions on Others

Because adherents of the my-way mindset are focused on achieving their own goals and meeting their own needs, their decisions and actions tend to revolve around their own self-interests. And because they believe that the other party is wrong, they need to win and not lose. They actually see the necessity of the other party losing. They have little interest in exploring how their decisions and actions affect others. This manifests itself during and following performance reviews by the my-way mindset supervisor or employee enforcing or implementing unilateral decisions and actions and not examining whether such decisions and actions negatively affect the other party.

31

Suppress My Own Feelings

My-way unilateralists view negative emotions in themselves and others as counterproductive, believing that negative emotions lead to the loss of control over a situation. By suppressing their own feelings of anger, frustration, anxiety, animosity, and so forth and channeling this emotional energy into scoring points, getting even, or regaining control, unilateralists can stay focused on achieving their goals. In performance reviews, one example of this might be either the supervisor or employee (or both) not expressing frustration, anger, anxiety, and so forth in constructive ways but instead using that emotional energy to focus on achieving goals and feeling victorious when scoring a point against the other side.

Prevent Others from Feeling Hurt by Covering Up, Withholding Information, and "Easing in" to Difficult or Sensitive Issues

Most of us call this not telling the whole truth or sugarcoating the message. Why do we tell incomplete truths or sugarcoat? We engage in these behaviors because we want to put people in a receptive mode so that we can get our point across and, therefore, achieve our goals. If people get overly defensive, anxious, or otherwise emotional, it makes it harder for us to maintain control in the conversation or relationship. So, instead of talking about the hard issues, we skirt around the topic, talk about the weekend or the weather, and eventually find a quiet way to get the person to do what we want them to do—sometimes without even bringing up the reason we stopped to talk to them in the first place.

Several years ago we worked with Steve, a VP of marketing, who made the extremely difficult decision to fire a member of his team. The employee just wasn't working out. Firing people wasn't a job that Steve liked doing—it wasn't in his nature to deliver such bad news—but he stepped up to the task nonetheless. So, on a Wednesday afternoon, Steve had a heart-to-heart conversation with Bill and told him that things weren't working out. Steve left the meeting feeling relieved that it was done. He could now focus his energy on other things. The next morning, however, Steve was very surprised to see Bill at his desk, working away, as if nothing had happened the day before. Steve approached Bill and asked him what he was doing at work, given their conversation the day before. Bill replied, with some confusion on his face, "I'm trying to make some headway on the issues we talked about. I heard you yesterday, and I'm going to try harder to hit the targets that you've set for me." Apparently, Steve was a bit too subtle for Bill. His sugarcoating the "you're-fired" message didn't translate into Bill actually realizing that he was being let go.

The classical approach to performance reviews is a great example of this enacting behavior. It's called the *sandwich technique*. Using sandwiching, a supervisor starts off the review by focusing on what the employee is doing well. After using the positive feedback to get the employee in a more receptive mood, the supervisor then brings up something the employee needs to improve—an area where the employee might feel uncomfortable. So, to address any employee discomfort and to keep her receptive to the supervisor's feedback and guidance, the supervisor ends the review by shifting to a positive note, perhaps remarking on how valuable the employee's contributions are to the team. In this framework the supervisor sandwiches the bad news among the good, hoping that the employee stays positive enough throughout the review for the supervisor to achieve his goals for the employee.

Don't Question Any of My Deeply Held Beliefs and Behavioral Patterns

Those who embrace the my-way mindset fundamentally believe that they are walking the right path in pursuit of the right goals. As a result, when things go wrong in a relationship, someone else is always to blame. Unilateralists aren't very introspective regarding their contribution to a misunderstanding or a problem—because they don't think that any part of it is their fault. Their behavior disrupts both interpersonal and professional relationships. My-way unilateralists confront a problem with reactions such as "You did this" or "You didn't do this right" or "If only you had done this differently" while failing to see their own contribution to the problem.

When preparing for and during a performance review, it's easy for a unilateralist supervisor or employee to see the problem in clear, black-and-white terms: I am doing everything okay, and the other party isn't. Without the willingness and therefore the capacity to examine their own involvement with a problem, however large or small, my-way unilateralists can't see it any other way. It's the *other* party that needs to change, not themselves.

Where It All Leads

When bringing together the governing values, underlying assumptions, and enacting behaviors of the my-way mindset, the results end up being pretty predictable. Because the my-way unilateralist has used a largely protective, insulating, and defensive suite of values, assumptions, and behaviors, there is very little opportunity for learning or growth by either party. New information isn't gathered, and when it does surface unilateralists tend to either ignore or reframe the information in a way that conforms to their viewpoint. And because unilateralists don't see the point or value in finding common ground or reaching an understanding with another person—except when this is the best way for them to achieve their goals—the relationship is destined to deteriorate if not disintegrate. This absence of learning—being closed off to new ideas and introspection—has its consequences.

Figure 2.2 lists some of the outcomes that result when the my-way mindset becomes the operating system for one or both parties. Oddly, while one would think that these negative outcomes would lead unilateralists to reconsider their beliefs or strategies, the opposite actually occurs. All of these negative results actually reinforce the unilateralists' viewpoint that they were right all along, that others are to blame for the problems before them, and that if only the world would see things their way all would be well! As you can see if you follow the reinforcing arrows in Figure 2.2, these negative outcomes lead my-way unilateralists to strengthen their commitment to the governing values and underlying assumptions and continue to bring the enacting behaviors into their relationships with others. While the unilateralist might feel self-satisfied in the short term, the my-way mindset remains a losing strategy over the long term.

Although unilateralists believe that sticking to the my-way mindset helps them achieve their goals, over the long run the results that they hope to achieve for themselves and others become harder to attain. The strange irony of the my-way mindset is that it only gives us the illusion of control. The harder we push using the my-way mindset, the less likely it is that our goals will be realized. Even if we experience a short-term "victory" using this approach (when we get our way), the array of negative consequences spinning out of this illusory victory lead to a longer-term erosion in our effectiveness, leadership, authority, credibility, and relationships with others. In the end, the my-way mindset is a losing strategy that is likely to take us further away from what we want.

Returning to performance reviews, given the stressful and often psychologically uncomfortable nature of the traditional performance review, it is natural that both the supervisor and employee might be inclined to move toward the my-way end of the mindset continuum we introduced in Chapter 2. As we've noted, a mindset that involves pursuing one's own self-interest, being right, minimizing negative feelings, being in control, focusing on winning and not losing, not being open to another's perspective, and so forth too often plays a central role in the approach that both supervisors and employees are likely to take during the performance review—especially if the focus is on delivering or receiving constructive feedback or bad news. And when that happens, anxiety and fear move to the forefront of the performance review, and insight, learning, and fundamental change take a back seat.

This is exactly what happened in Brenda and Tom's performance review. Both adopted a my-way mindset as they sat across the table from each other and, over the next hour, tended to talk at and past each other. Tom tried the sandwich technique (start with the good, move to the bad, and end with the good), but Brenda would have no part in what she rightly saw as a manipulative strategy. Tom started with the "good," but Brenda appeared unhappy. When Tom asked her what was wrong, she said, "Just go to page two—the bad stuff—you know that's why we're here."

So Tom switched gears and nervously brought up a specific performance problem from six months earlier. Brenda nearly went ballistic: "This is the first time I've heard of this," she shouted, "and it's hardly fair that you bring this up now and use it against me when I wasn't even aware of this so-called problem!"

Despite our attempts to slow things down and to get Tom and Brenda to hear each other and ask each other questions, neither side was truly receptive to a meaningful conversation. It would take more than a neutral facilitator to help these two people rebuild their relationship. To begin trusting each other, to begin working together toward shared goals, and to learn how to discover and explore common ground, they would each need to shift their mindset away from a my-way approach to one at the other end of the mindset continuum: collaboration.

As we have discussed in Chapter 1, the sources of fear and anxiety in performance reviews are many and varied. From the uncertainty of what will be revealed during a review to what's at stake for both parties to a mindset that's focused on defensiveness, winning not losing, and running away from embarrassment and vulnerabilities, it's not hard to see why the traditional performance review creates so much angst for both employees and supervisors. Fortunately, there is a better way—a mindset and approach that flips the my-way mindset and its related fears on its head and jumps deep into the pool of insight and learning. This is what we'll explore in the next chapter: an alternative pathway for truly transforming the relationship between employees and supervisors and performance reviews that builds a strong performance partnership, reduces fear, and leads to powerful insights and learning for all.

Let's turn away from the origins of fear in performance reviews to discover how to make our performance coaching conversations truly fearless!

THE COLLABORATIVE MINDSET

It's time we shift away from the counterproductive values, assumptions, and behaviors of the my-way mindset and toward a more constructive approach. While it is crucial to establish what *not* to believe and do as you plan for and conduct a performance review, for the review to be truly fearless it is necessary to adopt a new framework. This new framework, the collaborative mindset, is what we'll examine in Part 2.

Chapter 5 introduces the collaborative mindset by exploring what a fearless performance review might look and feel like. As with the my-way mindset in Part 1, the collaborative mindset is grounded in a set of governing values. We explore these in Chapter 6. And in Chapter 7 we guide you through the underlying assumptions based upon these governing values that help transport a performance review to a more collaborative coaching conversation.

Chapter 8 addresses how collaborative values and assumptions drive a suite of enacting behaviors that transform everyday unilateralist interactions (performance-related or not) to ones characterized by insight, learning, and discovery.

We finish Part 2 with Chapter 9 in which we demonstrate how the collaborative mindset can lead to the transformation that we promise. We'll walk you through an example of how the shift from the my-way to the collaborative mindset leads to profoundly different outcomes and a genuinely fearless review.

5

Transforming Relationships and Reviews Through the Collaborative Mindset

> *Quality is impossible if people are afraid to tell the truth.*
> —W. Edwards Deming

There's no doubt that performance reviews often raise uncomfortable truths that, for all of the reasons we cited in Chapter 1, contribute to higher levels of anxiety and fear in a supervisor as well an employee. The omnipresent my-way mindset that we introduced in Chapter 2 and explored in Chapters 3 and 4 is a key driver behind many of these fears and anxieties. At its foundation is a desire to avoid an embarrassment or threat, run for cover, escape blame, and simply avoid having to admit when one is wrong.

As we learned, however, this protective strategy is largely a defensive one that actually moves us further from what we want and the things that are important to us: self-confidence, strong and effective relationships with others, the ability to influence others' behavior, and movement toward achieving our personal and professional goals. It's clear that if we are to make performance reviews a productive process that leads to meaningful dialogue, insight, learning, and growth, then we need a different framework—an alternative mindset that leads us toward an entirely different set of outcomes than the my-way mindset does.

We introduced a mindset continuum in Chapter 2 that put the my-way mindset on the far left side. If we are looking for an alternative approach to managing our performance partnerships, navigating the performance review, and turning our employees into star performers, then we'll need to look toward the opposite end of that continuum—toward the end we call the collaborative mindset. Very broadly, this collaborative end of the continuum is characterized by the following sorts of beliefs: I have something to learn, people are doing their best, I only know part of the story, and we both can win. Imagine for a second that both the supervisor and employee adopted this mindset rather than its my-way unilateralist counterpart. Think about how each might prepare for and then navigate the performance review. Consider how the openness and receptivity of this collaborative approach might truly transform what is often a tense and difficult conversation into one in which both parties feel good about themselves and each other. The resulting conversation would involve both parties being fiercely committed to using the meaningful dialogue that emerges during the review to drive future performance toward the highest level.

The Outcomes from a Fearless Performance Review

So what might it look and feel like to have a truly fearless review where everything comes together to achieve the positive outcomes and feelings that both parties desire? In our consulting practice, when we ask employees and supervisors to describe the outcomes from an ideal performance review, this is what they tell us.

The Relationship Is Stronger

Because of the meaningful dialogue regarding what's working and what's not, what they each need from each other, the challenges each is experiencing, the pressures each might be facing, and so forth, there is a greater respect and trust between the supervisor and employee. Even when, and perhaps because, they have discussed the need for the employee to ramp up his performance or that the supervisor needs to be much clearer on setting expectations or providing more resource support, there is greater understanding about what each person needs from the other and a greater desire to become a true partner in the relationship.

They Speak Truthfully and Honestly to Each Other—No Undiscussables or Secrets

Honest dialogue lies at the core of a successful performance review. This means that people tell the truth in respectful ways—even when the truth may be uncomfortable to hear or say. In a fearless review each party comfortably raises issues that are crucial to discuss in order for learning and performance improvement to occur. With honest discussion, information and knowledge that may be critical to either the employee's or supervisor's understanding of the situation or its solution are openly shared, and, together, the supervisor and employee construct a plan of action.

There Is Greater Compassion and Understanding

In the ideal performance review there is genuine compassion for the other person's perspective, and this is especially true when there is disagreement or discord. Instead of blaming or defending, the supervisor and employee become curious and inquisitive: What might have caused this misunderstanding or performance challenge? What factors outside my awareness may have led to this problem? How can we come together to solve this problem?

As both parties work together to create a shared understanding of the challenge or problem, they do so with a sincere appreciation for the other person's circumstances, situation, barriers, pressures, and so forth. Compassion isn't about making excuses for or going easy on the other party; it's about a desire to understand the other person's situation and then work with that person to find a solution that addresses the underlying causes of a problem or challenge.

Problems and Challenges and Their Causes Are Identified and Addressed

Because there is honesty and a genuine dialogue about the employee's performance, there is compassion for the other person's viewpoint, the partnership between them is strong, and there are no undiscussables. Both parties raise issues and talk about what they really need to talk about to help the employee maintain, strengthen, or improve her performance. W. Edwards Deming once said, "Quality is impossible if people are afraid to tell the truth." In a fearless review no one is afraid of telling the truth!

Both the Employee and Supervisor Know and Understand More After the Conversation than They Each Did Before

If an ideal performance review involves a genuine dialogue and both parties telling the truth about where they are, where they need to go, and what they both need to do to get there, then new information and insights are likely to surface during this conversation. Even if the supervisor and employee get together on a regular basis to keep each other in the loop regarding expectations, needs, and performance outcomes, a deeper exploration of these matters during the more formal performance review will inevitably uncover new connections, perspectives, knowledge, and insights.

Each Party Is Deeply Committed to Performance Improvement

At the end of an ideal performance review—regardless of the performance issues raised and discussed, the challenges explored, the causes of performance problems examined, and so forth—the employee and the supervisor redouble their commitment to achieving great results together. The employee understands what to do to maintain, strengthen, or improve performance and leaves the review with a firm commitment to achieving the goals identified during the review. The supervisor understands how to support the employee in achieving the performance goals for the next performance cycle and is fiercely committed to doing whatever is necessary to help the employee move toward the agreed-upon goals.

All of these ideal performance review outcomes are available to each of us at any time. We don't need to master a script, memorize a list of phrases, follow a different process, or use a different performance review form. In fact, all we really need in order to move from a fear- or anxiety-inducing review toward a fearless review and the terrific outcomes described earlier is to embrace the values, assumptions, and behaviors found at the collaborative end of the mindset continuum. This is easy to propose but often difficult to enact, partly because it *is* more than just a new process, checklist, review form, and so forth; it involves adopting a new set of values and beliefs. And, as we all know from personal experience, adopting a new belief system is much harder than filling out a new form. Learning and enacting a new belief system is more challenging than simply demonstrating a new behavior; changing a specific behavior doesn't require us to change the way we see the world and ourselves in the world, while that is exactly what is required of us when we leave one belief system behind (my-way unilateralism) and then try to wrap our thinking and actions around a new one (collaboration).

For this reason, our prescription for a fearless performance review isn't like flipping a switch and suddenly arriving at the desired destination. Instead, it involves engaging in deep critical reflection and examining the lenses and filters through which we view ourselves and the world and then consciously shifting these lenses and filters to see ourselves and the world differently. To achieve fearless reviews, we'll need to learn to identify a new set of lenses and filters. When we've truly adopted this new framework, we'll be able to move our employees to star-performer status. Enter the collaborative mindset.

A Transformational Mindset for Achieving Great Results

In Chapter 2 we cited the work of Chris Argyris and Donald Schön when we introduced the my-way mindset (their Model 1) as the set of values, assumptions, and behaviors that contribute to fear-inducing reviews. Argyris and Schön identified an alternative theory-in-use that they found, unfortunately, to be less commonly practiced. Yet they discovered that when it was practiced, it led to a set of profoundly different and positive outcomes. They called this alternative approach Model II. Action Design and Schwarz renamed Model II the mutual learning model. We have expanded upon the work of these thinkers, blending their ideas with insights from William Isaacs, Susan Scott, and lessons learned through our own practice, to create a unique approach that we call the collaborative mindset.

As you'll see, the collaborative mindset offers a powerful set of interdependent values, assumptions, and enacting behaviors that, if successfully integrated into our thinking, decisions, and actions, is destined to change how we see ourselves and others in the world of performance management and reviews. Walking in this new direction is both easy (it's simply a new way of thinking!) and very difficult. Setting aside our default (and often defensive) my-way mindset during stressful situations in favor of this new perspective is challenging because it requires us to slow down, think critically and reflectively, steer clear of our defensive behaviors, and consciously use a new approach. It's like handling a dinner fork with our left hand if we're right handed: everything feels very different, but if we keep practicing, we eventually get the hang of it.

Figure 5.1 displays the collaborative mindset as it functions at the extreme right-hand side of the mindset continuum. If we are able to successfully understand and cultivate the values, assumptions, and behaviors that are part of this mindset, we are likely to undergo a transformation that moves us away from the unilateralist's "my-way-or-the-highway" perspective toward greater insight and learning that emerges from a "we're-in-this-together" perspective.

To varying degrees, these collaborative values, assumptions, and enacting behaviors are already part of who we are as individuals. We carry them within us into every relationship and situation. When we're around people we feel comfortable and safe with, when we agree with the other person we're talking with, when we seem to be working toward the same goals, it's easy to find our collaborative

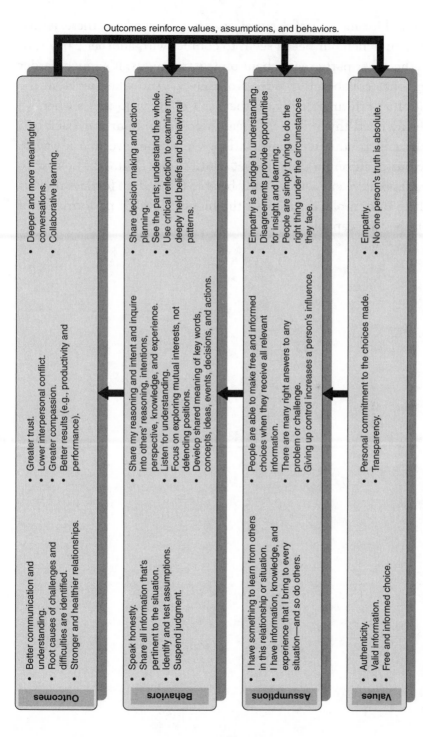

Outcomes reinforce values, assumptions, and behaviors.

Outcomes
- Better communication and understanding.
- Root causes of challenges and difficulties are identified.
- Stronger and healthier relationships.
- Greater trust.
- Lower interpersonal conflict.
- Greater compassion.
- Better results (e.g., productivity and performance).
- Deeper and more meaningful conversations.
- Collaborative learning.

Behaviors
- Speak honestly.
- Share all information that's pertinent to the situation.
- Identify and test assumptions.
- Suspend judgment.
- Share my reasoning and intent and inquire into others' reasoning, intentions, perspective, knowledge, and experience.
- Listen for understanding.
- Focus on exploring mutual interests, not defending positions.
- Develop shared meaning of key words, concepts, ideas, events, decisions, and actions.
- Share decision making and action planning.
- See the parts; understand the whole.
- Use critical reflection to examine my deeply held beliefs and behavioral patterns.

Assumptions
- I have something to learn from others in this relationship or situation.
- I have information, knowledge, and experience that I bring to every situation—and so do others.
- People are able to make free and informed choices when they receive all relevant information.
- There are many right answers to any problem or challenge.
- Giving up control increases a person's influence.
- Empathy is a bridge to understanding.
- Disagreements provide opportunities for insight and learning.
- People are simply trying to do the right thing under the circumstances they face.

Values
- Authenticity.
- Valid information.
- Free and informed choice.
- Personal commitment to the choices made.
- Transparency.
- Empathy.
- No one person's truth is absolute.

FIGURE 5.1 The Collaborative Mindset

Source: Adapted from the work of Chris Argyris, Donald Schön, Action Design, Roger Schwarz, William Isaacs, and Susan Scott

mindset. During stressful situations, however, where there is dis-agreement, when our needs seem to conflict with another party's, or when the other party seems bent on frustrating us, it's much harder to find that collaborative side of ourselves. And when we're in the midst of a performance review that isn't going well, that's when we especially need this mindset. It can help us find our way back to a healthy and productive conversation. Only when we find a way to move our position on the mindset continuum (Figure 2.1) closer to the collaborative end will we truly be able to conduct fearless reviews and help our employees achieve the highest level of performance of which they are capable.

THE GOVERNING VALUES OF THE COLLABORATIVE MINDSET

> *Out beyond the ideas of wrong-doing and right-doing, there is a field. I will meet you there.*
>
> —Rūmī, thirteenth-century Persian poet

The collaborative mindset's overarching purpose is insight and learning. Achieving this result requires a specific set of governing values and beliefs that, in a sense, represent the opposite set of values of the my-way mindset. Whereas my-way unilateralists assume a largely defensive array of values and beliefs, those who focus on collaboration tend to embrace values that create openness, explore new fields of information and knowledge, and build strong relationships. Let's take a closer look at each of the governing values of the collaborative mindset and, as we did with the my-way mindset, examine how each value is likely to influence both the supervisor's and employee's viewpoint and behaviors within their performance management partnership while preparing for and navigating the performance review itself.

Authenticity

Being honest with oneself and others, acting with integrity, demonstrating congruence between one's inner thoughts and external expressions: these are the ways in which the value of authenticity expresses itself. When we are authentic, we are being true to ourselves and outwardly acting in ways that are consistent with our actual intentions and motivations. In a strong partnership for performance between a supervisor and an employee, authenticity involves the supervisor speaking from the heart and behaving in ways that mirror his inner thoughts and intentions. For an employee authenticity means exactly the same thing: speaking honestly and not "putting on a face" or otherwise pretending to think or believe something that isn't true. When both parties are acting with authenticity, there is the highest level of honesty with neither assuming nor projecting a defensive image or posture.

Valid Information

This governing value (one of the defining values driving Argyris and Schön's Model 2) takes as its foundation the belief that critical thinking and effective decision making depend upon people having quality information readily available to them. Quality information is shared to empower all of the parties making a decision or taking an action to understand what they need to know in order to make a free and informed choice (see Free and Informed Choice, the next governing value). During a performance review this value requires that both the supervisor and employee actively seek out information and also share information with each other such that they both understand where things stand: what's working, what's not working, the causes behind success and failure, expectations for the future, and so forth. "Being on the same page" means that the supervisor and employee truly have a shared understanding of the employee's performance. Without this shared understanding, without exchanging valid information, it is difficult to find common ground on which to formulate the next steps. But *with* valid information clearly understood by both parties, identifying the next steps for the employee and the supervisor becomes far easier.

Free and Informed Choice

Free and informed choice, as with valid information, is another of Argyris and Schön's core values that profoundly informs a person's operating system of beliefs and assumptions about themselves and others. When people have valid information placed in front of them, they are much more able to make independent judgments and decisions that reflect an informed choice. Informed choices are made based upon having access to all of the information that's relevant to a particular decision. A free choice is one made without coercion by a person who has real choices rather than a single option that ultimately forces the decision.

What's crucial to understand about this governing value is that not all choices are equal. Some choices have significant positive consequences for the person doing the choosing, while others may have significant negative consequences. Simply knowing about the options or choices that are available and the consequences of each is what's important here. For example, in our relationship with another person we might have a preference that this person chooses a behavior that is aligned with our goals or needs. We can honor the free choice aspect of this governing value while also trying to influence the choice the person makes. We might offer the person an incentive to encourage her to choose what we think is the best behavior. We could further influence the person's choice by identifying disincentives that encourage the person to avoid some behaviors that work against our interests. In both cases of influence, however, the choice the person finally makes is still her own. Even though choices and any related consequences we might explore with another person are not equal from our perspective—or likely hers—the final choice is still a free one.

Within a performance review, for example, a supervisor might help an employee understand the performance choices that he is currently making (e.g., less-than-desirable performance) have problematic consequences for both the organization and the employee while encouraging him to make a *different* choice—one that has positive consequences for the organization and employee. The final choice

51

that the employee makes is an *informed* choice in that the employee understands the choices available to him and the consequences of each choice, and it is a *free* choice because the employee can choose from among the options—consequences and all.

Personal Commitment to the Choices Made

The collaborative mindset is based upon the premise that people are making free and informed choices, meaning that their decisions and actions are their own versus being imposed upon them by others. And when they do make a free and informed choice, people tend to have a higher degree of ownership and commitment to whatever decision they have made. Personal commitment—based upon another of Argyris and Schön's Model 2 core values—is a governing value of the collaborative mindset because without a personal commitment by all parties to a conversation, dialogue, decision, or course of action, one or more parties are likely to hold back.

At the end of a performance review the goal is to have both the employee and supervisor dedicated to the next steps that each will take to maintain or support the employee's performance in the future. If a personal commitment isn't present in either the employee or supervisor, then neither is likely to follow through on the agreed-upon next steps. When it is present, however, then both can be depended upon to follow through because the desire is coming from within versus being imposed from the outside.

Transparency

Transparency is important to the collaborative mindset because learning is only possible when people are speaking honestly and openly about what they know, understand, perceive, fear, and so forth. This governing value, along with the values of authenticity and valid information, ensures that critical information is out in the open and on the table. In an environment informed by transparency, people feel comfortable with open, honest, and direct communication in which there are no hidden agendas or undiscussables.

In relationships, transparency leads to people sharing their intentions and motivations in such a way that each person knows exactly where the others stand on an issue. No one is hiding out with his reservations in silence. Instead, everyone shares their reservations, doubts, and intentions. And when you have transparency, it's far easier for individuals and entire groups to decide what to do in any situation. Without transparency there is doubt and uncertainty (e.g., "I wonder what Steve is thinking? He seems troubled about something, but he's not saying anything. Is he behind this decision or not?"). In addition, without transparency either or both parties may end up making assumptions about the other party's intentions or motivations. With transparency, however, there is greater clarity about what each of us is thinking, where we are now, where we need to be, and what we might need to do to get to where we want to be.

Transparency is critical to performance reviews because both the employee and supervisor need to know—not guess at—the intentions and motivations of the other person. If either party is uncertain about what the other is driving at during the review, this uncertainty is likely to change the dynamic: either party might become guarded or circumspect. Without transparency, one or both parties might withhold information that the other party (whose motives or intentions are unclear) might use in ways that could be detrimental if revealed. With transparency it's perfectly clear what both the supervisor's and employee's intentions and motivations are because they actually state them. No secrets, no undiscussables, no hidden agendas—it's all out there for both parties to understand, discuss, and navigate.

Empathy

Desmund Tutu, the former archbishop of the Episcopal Church in the post-apartheid Republic of South Africa argues that "there is no hope without forgiveness." Tutu makes the case for understanding and having compassion for others' viewpoints, ideas, and actions. When individuals have empathy and compassion for others and their differing viewpoints and display a genuine interest in understanding another's perspective, anything is possible. In fact, it is only when we have empathy for those we disagree with that we can find common ground. Without empathy and compassion for the other party, what's the point of finding common ground? Why waste our time exploring mutual interests if we fundamentally don't care about the other side?

In some respects, empathy and compassion are the foundation of the collaborative mindset. For it is through empathy that we find our way to listening to others, caring about what they have to say, inquiring into their interests and perspectives, and finding common ground. Without empathy, none of this is possible because we simply don't care enough—or at all.

Empathy is crucial during the performance review because the supervisor has to bring a genuine interest in understanding the employee's viewpoint—especially when there is a performance problem. If the supervisor has no empathy for the employee's perspective, she will hear the employee's story about a performance problem as merely an excuse or rationalization for why things aren't where they need to be versus listening to the employee to begin exploring ideas and strategies to help find a way toward performance improvement. Similarly, if the employee has no empathy for or desire to understand the supervisor's perspective (e.g., "This is a waste of time. She has already made up her mind about me. She is just trying to get rid of me."), he is less likely to hear legitimate suggestions for improvement or be open to collaborating with the supervisor to find a way forward.

With empathy, compassion, and understanding by both the supervisor and the employee there is a genuine openness to hearing each other's viewpoints and a willingness to work through differences to find solutions that work for both parties. When there is appreciation for the other's perspective, especially when there is disagreement, the solution isn't too far off. It may not be easy, but at least the supervisor and employee are working together and respecting each other as they search for a fix to whatever performance challenge they are trying to resolve.

No One Person's Truth Is Absolute

One of the problems with adherents of the my-way mindset is that they deeply believe that they have the corner on truth. When you believe that you know "the" truth, you frankly aren't open to hearing others' viewpoints.

That's why this value is so foundational to the collaborative mindset. True collaboration hinges upon an openness to another person's perspective, which includes being open to their version of the truth. People who embrace the values of collaboration understand that each person's truth is a reflection of his own reality—how he perceives and interprets the world. Discovering a holistic, integrative truth only happens within a conversation where both parties are respecting each other's truths. If we all put our truths on the table and explore them together, we just might find a truly representative truth that captures and integrates the unique truths that each person contributes.

Let's be clear. This value doesn't require us to honor or agree with truths that are informed by ignorance, greed, revenge, retaliation, and so forth. It doesn't suggest that all truths should have equal weight when searching for a holistic truth. If someone's truth holds that other people are actively undermining her effectiveness, this value doesn't say that that truth is one that we should embrace. The value does encourage us to understand this person's truth, to explore what's behind this truth, and to perhaps help the person see that there are other truths involved in this situation that might help her see the world differently. By inviting people to share their respective truths while also being open to others' truths, we just might find a way to create a shared understanding about where we are and what we need to do next.

A key objective of every performance review is to discover the truth—the truth about where an employee's performance is currently and what the drivers of performance successes and failures are, the employee's understanding of his responsibilities for performance outcomes, and the role that the supervisor has played in enabling or sometimes even undermining the employee's success. The employee brings a version of the truth into the performance review, as does the supervisor. During performance reviews both supervisors and employees need to share their own truths while seeking out the truth of the other. By discovering, respecting, and exploring each other's truth, the holistic truth—a truth that's reflective of this journey of exploration—begins to emerge. If each person opens up his own respective truth to inspection and is willing to let his truth be influenced by the other, finding the holistic truth is inevitable.

With this value in effect, supervisors are willing to suspend their version of the truth (e.g., the employee is in the wrong job—there seems to be a person–skills mismatch) and reassess their understanding of the causes of an employee's performance challenges. At the same time, the employee might hear the supervisor's version of the truth, set aside personal conceptions (e.g., there is not much more that I can do to ramp up my performance to meet my boss's expectations), and become receptive to hearing the supervisor's truth. Somewhere in the space between these truths the way forward can be found. But this is likely to happen only when this core governing value is brought by each party into the performance conversation.

The thirteenth-century Persian poet Rūmī offers a poem that nicely sums up much of what the governing values of the collaborative mindset are trying to communicate:

> Out beyond the ideas of wrong-doing and right-doing,
> there is a field. I will meet you there.
> When the soul lies down in that grass,
> the world is too full to talk about
> language, ideas, even the phrase *each other*
> doesn't make any sense.
> "The Great Wagon," Chapter 4: Spring Giddiness, p. 36.[1]

The governing values of the collaborative mindset, like those of the my-way mindset, deeply influence how those who follow it interpret and engage the world. These values, in turn, shape a set of assumptions and enacting behaviors that lead to affirming outcomes that include strong and effective relationships centered on understanding, compassion, and learning.

CHAPTER 7

UNDERLYING ASSUMPTIONS OF THE COLLABORATIVE MINDSET

Could a greater miracle take place than for us to look through each other's eye for an instant?

—Henry David Thoreau

If we define assumptions as the stories that we tell ourselves in order to help us interpret the way the world and people operate, then it's fair to say that those who use a collaborative mindset tell themselves stories that are very different than those told by my-way unilateralists. These assumptions create openness and receptivity to new ideas and information, which enhances understanding and strengthens relationships—especially when there is disagreement. Let's examine how the values of the collaborative mindset emerge in a powerful set of underlying assumptions that are in stark contrast to those of the my-way mindset.

I Have Something to Learn from Others in This Relationship or Situation

The governing values of the collaborative mindset contribute to a genuine openness to others that naturally leads into this assumption. Those whose orientation is toward collaboration enter every relationship and situation—even challenging ones—with the assumption that they have something to learn. And, not surprisingly, they do! Every time.

I Have Information, Knowledge, and Experience that I Bring to Every Situation—and So Do Others

This is another assumption based upon openness and receptivity to others' viewpoints. Collaborators honor the information, knowledge, and experience that they bring to each situation and are ready to honor and respect what others bring to these situations. They recognize the value of bringing diverse information, knowledge, and experience together to create a holistic understanding of every situation.

People Are Able to Make Free and Informed Choices When They Receive Relevant Information

This assumption brings together two of the governing values of the collaborative mindset to yield a powerful synergy. Combining the values of *valid information* and a *free and informed choice* enables people to make informed decisions, which, in turn, leads to a high level of personal commitment to these decisions (another of this mindset's governing values).

There Are Many Right Answers to Any Problem or Challenge

Collaborators embrace the idea of *equifinality*, which means that there are many paths to the goal, not just the one that is known to you or preferred by you. This underlying assumption posits that while we individually might believe that there is one right answer to any given problem or challenge, in reality there may be dozens of right answers. The path we finally take toward the goal emerges from an exploration, through conversation, of these many possibilities to find the one that seems to be the best fit for our circumstances. If we set aside preconceived notions that our truth is the only one, that we must win, and that others are wrong (all reflecting the my-way unilateralist's values and assumptions), we are free to discover, by interacting with others, new pathways that would otherwise be unknown to us.

Giving Up Control Increases a Person's Influence

Those who embrace the collaborative mindset intuitively understand that when we use our titles or authority to get what we want or when we try to control another person, the very act of exerting control, authority, or title actually diminishes our ability to influence others' behavior. But when we let go of the need to control others or the outcomes of a situation, the power of our influence actually grows. Especially when the relationship matters as much as or more than the outcome, influence strategies are far more effective than command and control behaviors. Forcing people to do things often leads to resistance, anger, and even deception (e.g., people might pretend to go along, but in reality they are walking in the opposite direction).

By giving up control and shifting our energy to having influence we are forced to use an entirely different set of behaviors, skills, and strategies. Instead of telling, we listen. Instead of forcing or pushing, we invite and inquire. Instead of focusing on rewards, threats, or punishments, we focus on paying attention and learning the motivations and intentions of others. And when we do all of this—when we listen, invite, inquire, pay attention, and learn—our power and influence actually grow. It is said that we have less control and more power than we realize, and this key underlying assumption of the collaborative mindset helps us see how this is true.

This assumption was made clear to Jeff, one of the authors, many years ago. When Jeff was 13 years old, he was elected by his peers to be a patrol leader in Boy Scout Troop 130 in Menomonie, Wisconsin. Jeff was ecstatic! It was his first leadership role in life. His election meant that his peers admired him, and the gift of that admiration, Jeff reasoned, was the ability to make decisions, give people direction, and, most importantly, be in charge of things! As the Boy Scout troop's first camping trip after his election approached, Jeff was filled with anticipation: this trip would give him his first opportunity to demonstrate and prove his value as a leader.

On the first day of the camping weekend, the patrol hiked into the woods, located the camping grounds, and had just set their backpacks down when Jeff's sense of leadership kicked into high gear. He started by telling Steve where to build the fire, Bill where to pitch the tents, John how to gather the best firewood, Mark how to set up the cooking area and prepare the patrol's lunch, and so on until the patrol's campground was alive with activity—with Jeff as the master conductor! Jeff felt powerful and effective as he offered his fellow scouts his wisdom, insights, and directions toward achieving a great camping experience. Unfortunately, the *great* part of the camping experience quickly evaporated. By early afternoon on the first day of the camping weekend, as Jeff found himself abandoned by his patrol in the middle of the woods, it suddenly struck him that something wasn't right; what he was doing wasn't working. He realized that his title as patrol leader and how he interpreted this role (e.g., telling and yelling!) were actually getting in the way of his ability to be a good leader. It dawned on him that he had jettisoned the behaviors that had gotten him elected to his post (e.g., being a friend and a good listener, sharing his experience, and so forth) and replaced these behaviors with a suite of command and control strategies that his patrol found irritating. It was clear that his patrol had begun to have second thoughts about its decision to promote him to this leadership position.

Fortunately for Jeff (and the rest of his patrol!), he was able to translate this sudden insight into behavioral change. He was able to give up the need to control and shift back to using influence. He became the good guy again, and peace returned to the camping trip. But it was a close call. If he hadn't been paying attention to the actual effects of his controlling behavior, he might not have realized that the strategy was ineffective. Jeff's life wasn't totally transformed by this experience. Over the years he has occasionally dipped his toe back into the waters of command and control, but each time he does, he rediscovers the lessons of his first camping trip as a patrol leader and tries to make the journey back toward using influence.

Empathy Is a Bridge to Understanding

As we said in our introduction to the governing values of the collaborative mindset, empathy and compassion are at the core of the collaborative approach. Without empathy and compassion it's nearly impossible to be open to other people's perspectives, appreciate their situations, or listen to divergent viewpoints. Empathy gives us the opportunity to discover common ground by helping us bridge the gap between our experience and perspective and those of others.

Disagreements Provide Opportunities for Insight and Learning

When people are on the same page, when they agree wholeheartedly, when they see eye to eye, very little learning actually takes place. Insight and learning only occur when what we experience in the moment conflicts, clashes with, or expands our awareness beyond what we know or take for granted. This underlying assumption recognizes that it is when we disagree with another person that we are compelled to think in new ways, look in new directions, and consider new perspectives. And through this exploration of divergent thoughts comes the possibility of insight and learning.

People Are Simply Trying to Do the Right Thing Under the Circumstances They Face

This underlying assumption often poses the most challenges for us—even for those who are collaborators at heart. When we accept this assumption, we are accepting that the actions that people take are, in part, a function of the environment in which they operate. The premise of this assumption is that on any given day people are simply trying to do the right thing to find the best way forward.

But doesn't this condone or at least excuse bad behavior? Does this give poor performers or difficult people a free ride to do whatever they wish—because they are doing their best, given their circumstances? This assumption doesn't say that people's behavior is appropriate or desirable, it just suggests that a person's behavior needs to be seen within its context to better understand why someone would engage in behaviors that might be harmful to others or even to themselves.

Rather than judging undesirable behavior and writing the person responsible off as a jerk or beyond redemption, the focus of a collaborative mindset shifts to better understanding why someone would act in such a way. If the goal is to influence the person to behave differently in the future (whether the behavior is performance related or simply inappropriate in a situation), then we need to try to understand why this person would make such undesirable choices and attempt to influence his future decision making. The process of using influence begins with exploring and understanding the context and origins of the person's behavior (the factors that contributed to the person making the choice), asking questions about his intentions and motivations, discussing with the person the range of possible alternative choices available to him, and even identifying potentially negative consequences that could result from continuing to behave in counterproductive ways and positive consequences that could result from behaviors that are more aligned with the needs of others.

Within a performance review this assumption would have us suspend our judgments about an employee who is doing the wrong things and instead explore the reasons why the employee might feel that such behaviors or outcomes are acceptable. And when we explore the array of possible causes behind the employee's behavior, we might just find that we might have played a role in creating the employee's undesirable behaviors or outcomes. Perhaps we assumed that he knew what the performance objective was. Maybe we didn't take the time to assess the skill or knowledge level of the performer. We might not have paid close enough attention earlier to the employee's performance or given him timely feedback on his work. This isn't to suggest that the employee's bad behavior is our fault (finding fault isn't productive here), it just means that if we want to understand the effects (behaviors and outcomes), we need to better understand their causes. And blaming the employee (or ourselves for that matter) for the behaviors we don't want doesn't help. In fact, it actually hinders our search for solutions because it prevents us from digging deeper into why things have gone wrong.

In concert with the governing values of the collaborative mindset, these underlying assumptions provide powerful lenses and filters that focus people's attention and profoundly influence how they view and interpret the world around them. Collectively, these values and assumptions create an openness to divergent perspectives that can lead to insights that can lead to learning—all of which can lead to people changing their viewpoints, perspectives, opinions, and judgments in ways that reflect a more complete understanding of the world.

8

ENACTING BEHAVIORS FOR COLLABORATION

> *If there is any one secret of success, it lies in the ability to get the other person's point of view and see things from his angle as well as your own.*
>
> —Henry Ford, American industrialist

While both values and behaviors influence the way collaborators understand and interpret the world, their actual behaviors are what matter most. As displayed in Figure 5.1, the behaviors that emerge from the values and assumptions of the collaborative mindset represent a powerful suite of actions that lead to a profoundly different set of outcomes when compared with the behaviors that stem from the my-way mindset.

Speak Honestly

This behavior, crucial to the collaborative mindset, involves speaking with integrity, telling the truth in a respectful way, and using the power of our voice and words to build up rather than tear down. When we speak honestly, we speak from the heart in ways that work to inform and strengthen others' and our relationships. Our authenticity and genuineness can enlighten, refresh, startle, and disarm. Speaking honestly means speaking truthfully when we see something that isn't right and speaking respectfully when we disagree with others.

A performance review is effective only when both parties are willing and able to speak honestly and sometimes courageously. This means surfacing disagreements in ways that lead to understanding rather than defensiveness. Using this behavior during a review, a supervisor doesn't sugarcoat performance problems but instead surfaces them in ways that encourage a dialogue with the employee to better understand how to turn things around. An employee might speak honestly about needing more direction, support, or feedback from the supervisor and do this in a way that doesn't put the supervisor on the defensive. When both parties are speaking honestly, the hard issues are raised and discussed. Both know what is before them, and they work together to find lasting solutions to the performance challenges.

Share All Information That's Pertinent to the Situation

As we discussed earlier when we explored the governing values and underlying assumptions of the collaborative mindset, people can only make informed choices or decisions when they are aware of and have access to all of the information they need. This requires us to actively participate in dialogue with each other—to say what we're thinking and what we know. Sharing all pertinent information also involves saying, "I don't have an opinion" or "I don't have anything to add to the discussion" rather than remaining silent (and causing people to wonder, at best, if we are sharing all information that we know or, at worst, to make assumptions about what we're thinking or what our intentions are).

In a performance review this involves the supervisor and employee sharing all valid information, enabling them to make free and informed decisions about what needs to happen next. If an employee doesn't share data about a past performance failure that the supervisor may not know about, the supervisor won't have the chance to explore with the employee the causes of the failure and discuss possible solutions. The result may be that the performance problem continues (perhaps flying under the supervisor's radar), and, even if no one else knows, the employee's performance suffers.

If, due to time constraints or a feeling that "she should already know this," a supervisor fails to share his vision of the work team's future or the employee's position, then the employee could miss an important expectation that might limit her ability to hit the performance target to the supervisor's satisfaction. Without this crucial information driving the employee's behavior, the supervisor might begin to wonder about her commitment because the performance results aren't quite where they need to be.

In order to become star performers, employees need to have near-complete knowledge of where they are at in terms of performance, where they need to be in the future, and what actions they can take to move toward that goal. This is something that they can't usually do alone—supervisors must play an active part in contributing to employees' knowledge base. Meeting or exceeding desired performance outcomes involves creating a shared understanding of an employee's performance environment, and that can only happen when there is a rich exchange of information between the employee and the supervisor.

Identify and Test Assumptions

When we observe those around us making statements, taking actions, and making decisions, it's easy to speculate about their intentions and motivations. We fall into this pattern because our brain needs clarity and closure. We need to know what to do in any given situation, and when we don't have all the data in front of us, we make things up; we create a story that explains things for us. Once we have the story figured out, we are then able to decide how to respond.

Assumptions are the stories that we create about others when we don't have complete knowledge about their behaviors or intentions. Our stories help us explain why Cindy leaves the room when we are making a presentation, Bill missed a deadline on a critical project, Ashley always misinterprets what we say, John is routinely late for work, and the team has been consistently missing its performance targets for the past six months. In each of these scenarios we need a story that explains these behaviors to enable us to know what we should do next: Do I stop inviting Cindy to my meetings? Do I stop working with Bill? Do I slow things way down and spell things out for Ashley? Is it time to let John go? Maybe the team needs a shakeup in leadership?

This enacting behavior first involves identifying when you have created a story (made an assumption). That's not as easy as it sounds; the stories that we tell ourselves are so good that we forget they are stories and simply accept them as facts: Steve is undermining me in front of the group because he doesn't like my ideas. Too often, the first step to surfacing and testing our assumptions—*identifying* our assumptions—is never taken. We just simply go with our story—and stick to it. We then actively seek out data that reinforces our story and the beliefs we formed about the other person's behavior, and we ignore any data that conflicts with the neat story that we've invented. This is what we call "self-sealing" and "self-fulfilling" thinking: we don't let new information into our consciousness (instead, we just look for confirming information), and we only see what we expect to see.

Figure 8.1 displays a powerful diagram that reveals how the stories we tell ourselves influence our judgments and actions—and offers insights into how we can successfully stop the process before we run with our story and end up getting things quite wrong. Called the *ladder of inference*, this diagram (based upon the work of Chris Argyris, Peter Senge, Rick Ross, William Isaacs, and others) shows how quickly we can take an event and, through a series of cognitive and emotional leaps up the ladder, find ourselves in a

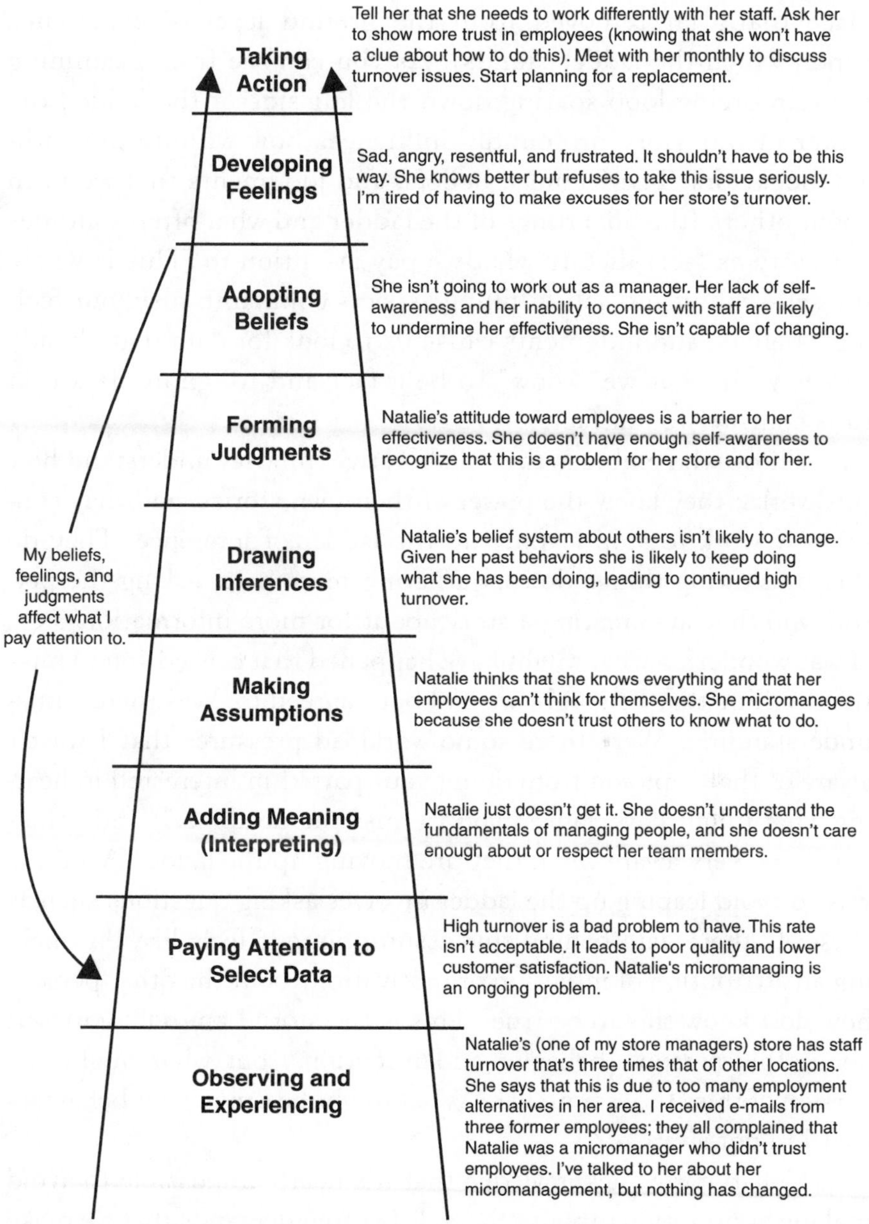
Taking Action
Tell her that she needs to work differently with her staff. Ask her to show more trust in employees (knowing that she won't have a clue about how to do this). Meet with her monthly to discuss turnover issues. Start planning for a replacement.
Developing Feelings
Sad, angry, resentful, and frustrated. It shouldn't have to be this way. She knows better but refuses to take this issue seriously. I'm tired of having to make excuses for her store's turnover.
Adopting Beliefs
She isn't going to work out as a manager. Her lack of self-awareness and her inability to connect with staff are likely to undermine her effectiveness. She isn't capable of changing.
Forming Judgments
Natalie's attitude toward employees is a barrier to her effectiveness. She doesn't have enough self-awareness to recognize that this is a problem for her store and for her.
Drawing Inferences
Natalie's belief system about others isn't likely to change. Given her past behaviors she is likely to keep doing what she has been doing, leading to continued high turnover.
My beliefs, feelings, and judgments affect what I pay attention to.
Making Assumptions
Natalie thinks that she knows everything and that her employees can't think for themselves. She micromanages because she doesn't trust others to know what to do.
Adding Meaning (Interpreting)
Natalie just doesn't get it. She doesn't understand the fundamentals of managing people, and she doesn't care enough about or respect her team members.
Paying Attention to Select Data
High turnover is a bad problem to have. This rate isn't acceptable. It leads to poor quality and lower customer satisfaction. Natalie's micromanaging is an ongoing problem.
Observing and Experiencing
Natalie's (one of my store managers) store has staff turnover that's three times that of other locations. She says that this is due to too many employment alternatives in her area. I received e-mails from three former employees; they all complained that Natalie was a micromanager who didn't trust employees. I've talked to her about her micromanagement, but nothing has changed.

FIGURE 8.1 The Ladder of Inference

Source: Based upon the work of Chris Argyris, Peter Senge, Rick Ross, and William Isaacs

place that's far removed from the ground level of experience (upon which the ladder stands). As you can see from examining the reinforcing loop soaring down the left side of the ladder, the power of our story profoundly influences how we interpret others' behaviors. The feelings, beliefs, and judgments that we form about others (the final rungs of the ladder and what often solidifies our story as fact) dictate what we pay attention to. This is where the self-sealing and self-fulfilling aspects come into play: our feelings, beliefs, and judgments cause us to look for data that already agrees with what we "know" to be a fact and to ignore data that runs contrary to our facts.

Those who embrace the collaborative mindset understand how this works; they know the power of their own stories, and they consciously work to stop leaping up the ladder of inference. They do this by slowing things down, gathering more data, asking the person who they are creating a story about for more information (e.g., "I was wondering what might have happened that caused you to miss the deadline that I thought we had both agreed to. Was there a misunderstanding? Were there some workload pressures that I wasn't aware of that kept you from doing your part? I'm interested in hearing what might have caused you to miss the deadline.") and generally being very aware when they are moving up the ladder. A simple way to avoid leaping up the ladder involves asking questions such as these: Is there data behind this assumption? It feels like I'm making an attribution of intention or motivation about the other person; how do I know this to be true? This is the story I am telling myself about this person's behavior and intentions, but what might her version of this story sound like? What might be driving her behaviors that I'm not aware of?

Collaborators acknowledge that it's nearly impossible to avoid making assumptions about others. Life often demands that we make assumptions just to get through the day. The difference between a my-way unilateralist and a collaborator is that the collaborator is aware of the story and is willing to test it out. The unilateralist just runs with the story because it explains things; in their view, running with the story that they've invented makes things a lot simpler. Although it's likely that the unilateralist's story is entirely or at least partially wrong, he doesn't pause long enough to check things out. And, in the end, because the unilateralist sticks with his version of the story, the outcomes usually just confirm the unilateralist view of the world—another example of self-fulfilling, self-sealing processes at work.

How does this enacting behavior play out during a performance review? When a supervisor is actively testing assumptions that she makes about the employee, the supervisor is more likely to gather *real* data and less likely to create and run with a story about an employee's intentions, motivations, and behaviors. With valid information and less storytelling, the supervisor, in turn, is more likely to base her judgments and actions on hard data. It's fairer to the employee, likely to lead to more meaningful conversations, apt to enhance the quality of performance improvement planning, and destined to increase the likelihood of better performance results. When an employee similarly tests assumptions rather than inventing and running with a story about the supervisor's intentions and motivations, the employee is more likely to base his judgments about the supervisor upon real data and is more likely to take actions that reflect a better understanding of the supervisor's viewpoint.

Suspend Judgment

In our normal interactions with others we tend to make quick judgments about what others have said or done. We form judgments about others' statements or actions that tell us that the other person is good, bad, right, wrong, foolish, bold, brutish, bullying, caring, and so forth often without hard data behind our conclusions. Often these judgments form as a result of the assumptions that we have embedded in our stories that help us understand another person's behavior. As you saw in the ladder of inference (Figure 8.1), the judgment rung is near the top of the ladder—it represents the conclusions we form based upon all of the interpretations, assumptions, and inferences we have made about another person.

With the collaborative mindset driving our behaviors, however, instead of rushing to judgment, we question our stories, test out our assumptions, and suspend our judgments about others. When we suspend our judgments, we put our judgments on hold—putting enough distance between our judgments and ourselves to ensure that we are free from having to *act* upon or be influenced by them. The space and time that's created when we suspend judgment allows us to explore other information and consider alternative explanations of someone's behavior.

If, however, we treat our judgments about others as truths, we tend to limit our data gathering or, worse, only look for data that confirms our judgments. This is called *confirmation bias* because we look for information that confirms what we have already decided about another person. The actions we can take to escape rushing to judgment and avoid confirmation bias mirror what we identified as steps for testing assumptions in the previous behavior: be aware that it's happening, slow the process down, consider alternative interpretations that might lead to different judgments, and ask questions.

Prior to and during performance reviews it's easy for both the employee and supervisor to make up their minds in advance about the other person (e.g., "She is dead-set on getting rid of me. He isn't open to hearing bad news. She avoids taking responsibility for her part of any problem. He is a freeloader—just coasting on the team's coattails."). By suspending judgment prior to and during the performance review, however, both the supervisor and employee are open to additional data that might enable them to reach a different judgment than their initial inclination. In the end the supervisor and employee may conclude that their initial judgments (e.g., "She is trying to fire me! He isn't interested in solutions, only blame!") are correct—but neither rushes to these conclusions. And when they each slow things down, the holistic truth is more likely to be discovered.

Share My Reasoning and Intent, and Inquire Into Others' Reasoning, Intentions, Perspective, Knowledge, and Experience

This enacting behavior enables others to see how we reached the conclusion and judgment that we did and allows others to then explore areas of our reasoning where they might have reasoned differently. When we explain to others why we think the way that we do about something or why we made a statement we did, it enables them to better understand the basis for our words and actions and our purpose or reasons for doing something. The second half of this behavior involves us actively inquiring into others' reasoning, intentions, perspectives, and so forth to better understand *how* they arrived at the conclusions and judgments that they did. When we genuinely inquire into others' reasoning and intentions, we are far more able to understand and appreciate what lies behind their words and actions. Collaboration naturally evolves from the rich dialogue that emerges from this two-way sharing of reasoning and intentions and appreciation of divergent experience and backgrounds.

When there's a disagreement between people, it's easy for each party to slip into assertions and declarations that make a case for being right. We thrust out our argument, expecting that the volume, intensity, or clarity of our statement by itself is enough to sweep others into agreement with us. Unfortunately for us, this rarely works. Simply pushing harder in an argument or raising the decibels isn't likely to convince someone to agree with us.

When we approach disagreements from a collaborative mindset perspective, however, we lower the volume and intensity and move beyond the argument to explain how we arrived at our position. When we explain to others the cognitive steps we took, the information we considered, the facts we rolled over in our minds, our experience with the issue, and so forth, it allows others to better understand and perhaps appreciate the journey we made to arrive at our judgment or position. Actively inquiring into others' reasoning paths helps us understand their cognitive and/or emotional journey to better appreciate why they believe and assert what they do. Taken together, the sharing of one's own reasoning and the inquiring into the other's reasoning opens both parties up to a genuine dialogue about the issue being considered; it allows each person to influence the other's reasoning to such an extent that both are more open to changing their minds, perhaps ending up with different judgments or positions. That's the power of sharing our respective reasonings: it allows others to examine and actually influence how we think. Each of us, in the end, might still hold on to our original positions or judgments, but at least now others better understand where we're coming from—even if they continue to disagree with us.

Another important aspect of this particular behavior involves sharing our intentions with others. When we are transparent with others about what we are trying to accomplish in taking the actions that we do, it prevents people from having to guess at our intentions. As we discussed during our exploration of the behavior *identify and test assumptions*, when people don't have information available to them, they make it up! So, if we don't share our intentions with others, they are likely to create a story about why we are doing what we're doing. Do yourself a favor: be very clear about why you are taking the actions you are taking, and don't give people the chance to invent something out of thin air.

Sharing reasoning and intentions and exploring others' reasoning and intentions play a crucial role in helping make the performance review a fearless one. When the supervisor lays out exactly what he is trying to do (intentions), what actions he is proposing the employee take to solve a performance problem, and why he is suggesting these actions (reasoning), the employee doesn't have to guess or create a story that explains the supervisor's actions or intentions. Rather than just telling the employee to do something, the supervisor explains the reasons why he believes that the employee should take these actions. At the same time, the supervisor might inquire about what happened to cause the performance problem to begin with. Without judging the employee or asking the employee to defend herself, the supervisor inquires into the employee's reasoning path. The supervisor might say something like, "I'd like to explore the factors that led to the problem we've been discussing. I'm curious— could you walk me through what you were thinking when you decided to respond in that way to the customer? I'm not asking you to defend what you did; I'm just interested in exploring your thought process. And then, if it seems appropriate, we can figure out how best to get you thinking things through in a different way."

When an employee explains why he took the actions that he did, it allows the supervisor to understand the employee's reasoning path and then, if necessary, influence that reasoning path in the future. Because one of the goals of performance reviews is to develop a plan for maintaining or strengthening performance in the future, examining and influencing the employee's reasoning path may be a critical step that a supervisor needs to take to affect a sustainable shift in the employee's thinking and behavior.

Listen for Understanding

Collaboration depends upon good communication, and good communication involves more than simply exchanging information. Effective communication involves the creation of understanding— the creation of shared meaning. And for understanding and shared meaning to occur within a relationship there needs to be more than just sending messages back and forth. This is where listening comes in—listening for understanding.

The collaborative mindset depends upon the skill of active listening with a focus on creating a shared understanding and appreciating another's perspective. Active listening involves being assertive when it comes to gathering information from people about what they are saying and also about what they are not saying—exploring what thoughts and emotions underlie the words of others. This means paying attention to the meta-language of others: their vocal tone and intensity, the pace of their speech, and their body language. The value of focusing on the metalanguage is to gain a holistic understanding of the other person's message. Just paying attention to the words is not sufficient to extract meaning from another's message.

Active listening, however, doesn't just stop with the listener gathering visual, vocal, and verbal data. To avoid creating a story about the intentions of the other person around the data that you've collected, it's crucial that you share and verify your understanding. This is called mirroring, reflecting, and paraphrasing, and it's a crucial step in the process. It allows you to let the other person know what you heard and observed and any insight you've gained through these perceptions. Reflective listening enables the other person to confirm or disconfirm and correct your understanding of what you heard or observed. Without this step that verifies understanding, you haven't created shared meaning and you don't have communication. For this reason, active listening is an essential tool in the collaborator's toolkit.

Fear-inducing reviews are notorious for lots of talking or even lecturing and very little listening. To reduce fear and facilitate collaborative problem solving that leads toward improvement, both the supervisor and employee need to become active listeners. They each need to engage in a genuine back-and-forth exchange of perspectives—mirroring and reflecting, verifying and clarifying as they go along—to cultivate a shared understanding of whatever they are discussing. While active listening slows things down and takes time, the alternative is not having a shared understanding and potentially continuing the misunderstanding, confusion, and conflict.

Focus on Exploring Mutual Interests, Not Defending Positions

In the book *Getting to Yes*, a groundbreaking work on negotiating your way to win-win outcomes, authors Roger Fisher and William Ury, argue that successful conflict management and negotiation involves focusing on our own and others' interests rather than on positions.

The problem with people taking and defending positions when they disagree is that, almost by definition, the positions between two people often represent opposites—sometimes in the extreme—and that these positions *never* intersect. In other words, they are perceived to be mutually exclusive: both cannot be true at the same time. As a result, people argue over whose position is best, with neither side giving ground because each person wants to win and each believes that his position is the correct one.

Within the collaborative mindset we move away from focusing on positions (and holding, defending, and protecting our positions) and instead focus on better understanding and sharing the interests behind our positions and exploring the interests of others. Our interests and the interests of the other party reflect the underlying needs and desires that are on the table in a given situation. There is an opportunity inherent in this exploration of interests: they almost always intersect, creating the possibility of finding common ground. When both parties focus on sharing and exploring each other's interests, it is far easier to find a solution that meets both parties' needs.

Performance reviews can sometimes end up focusing on positions (e.g., "I'm right, and you're wrong. This is the way you need to do this. Here is what needs to happen next. What were you thinking when you did that?"). The result is often tension, defensiveness, and arguments about whose position will win out in the end. It doesn't have to be this way. Using this enacting behavior within a performance review would involve both the supervisor and employee moving beyond the duality of black and white, I win and you lose, toward a deeper exploration of the expectations, goals, and perceptions that each of them bring into the relationship. By using a variety of enacting behaviors (e.g., speaking honestly, sharing pertinent information, suspending judgment, sharing reasoning and intentions, and active listening) they can each begin to understand where the other person is coming from, discover areas of common ground, and learn how they might be able to move forward. And throughout and because of this free-flowing dialogue between the two of them, learning occurs. By exploring the field of mutuality, each person discovers something new about herself and the other party. Whereas my-way unilateralists aggressively defend and protect their positions during a performance review (which profoundly limits their understanding, agreement, and learning), collaborators find ways to build bridges between each other's interests to strengthen their relationship and enable the employee to become a star performer.

Develop Shared Meaning of Key Words, Concepts, Ideas, Events, Decisions, and Actions

It's hard to have a conversation about something if the two people in the conversation are talking about different things. But doesn't this happen all of the time? Isn't it true that many of our disagreements result from not having a shared understanding of the problem—of what actually happened and when, of who said what, of the causes of a problem, the expectations of each other, the specifics of a solution, and so forth? Before we can agree upon a solution we first need to agree upon what the issue or problem is and have a shared understanding of its causes.

Creating shared meaning and understanding regarding specific dates, times, places, and key words ensures that relevant information is available to all and that we're on the same page. When we have a shared understanding of key events and their causes, we are more able to have an informed discussion about the issues before us. And when we agree on the meaning of key terms such as agreement, quality, learning, consensus, conflict, opportunity, commitment, hard worker, and motivated, we work from a shared understanding of the word or idea rather than drawing upon different meanings of these words and going off in different directions.

Because performance reviews involve establishing a shared understanding of where the employee is today (and why) and what he needs to do to maintain, strengthen, or improve performance in the future, getting agreement on the definition of these fundamental issues is paramount. When the supervisor brings up an employee's performance success, she needs to zero in on the specifics of the success such that the employee knows what the supervisor is talking about. Once they are both on the same page, they can then explore what enabled the event to be successful and identify steps to replicate such positive outcomes for the future. Similarly, if either the supervisor or employee raises a performance problem, they both need to ensure that they have a shared understanding of the issue before they can establish a shared understanding of the causes. In each case both parties need to be willing to invest time in building agreement on these things before moving toward solutions and strategies.

If an employee says to the supervisor, "The problem I'm having is that you aren't giving me adequate support," then the two of them have to define what adequate support is—what it looks like—before they mutually decide what actions the supervisor might need to take in relation to supporting the employee.

If a supervisor says to the employee, "I don't really see a high level of engagement and ownership from you on this job. I need you to step up your level of commitment," they both need to discuss what words like engagement, ownership, and commitment mean in observable and measurable ways. Without establishing agreement on the meaning of these terms the employee isn't likely to have a clear idea of the supervisor's expectations, and even the supervisor might not be sure when the right level of engagement, ownership, or commitment are present in the employee's work.

Share Decision Making and Action Planning

When we act unilaterally, we attempt to impose our ideas, actions, and answers onto others. This mindset preserves the black-and-white, I'm right–you're wrong mentality, leaving no room for others' ideas and certainly not building any measure of commitment from others toward the imposed ideas or solutions. In contrast, collaboration involves working together with others to jointly decide on what will happen and how to implement the decision—even when one or both parties *could* be unilateral. This might involve the supervisor setting aside and not relying upon her title and authority and shifting instead toward influence and collaboration. Those who follow the collaborative mindset focus on building ownership and personal commitment to decisions and actions (a governing value) because if people's hearts aren't invested in a course of action, they're less likely to be there to help problem solve when things aren't going well.

If you're a manager or supervisor, you always have the option, in the end, to impose a unilateral decision or action on others. And sometimes acting unilaterally may be warranted, especially when there is an urgent situation: someone's safety is at risk, there's a need to move quickly to avoid or solve a problem, there's a gaping hole in quality or productivity, and so forth. But a manager or supervisor can still approach such unilateral decisions from a collaborative perspective by explaining the circumstances and one's intentions and promising to revisit the decision or action following the passing of the crisis or problem. And then, after the intensity of the moment and the need to act quickly passes, the manager or supervisor can bring people together to talk about the process, the decision, the causes of the situation, and ideas for avoiding such situations in the future. So even when we need to act unilaterally, we can do it in a collaborative way!

During a performance review, a supervisor should approach a performance problem in a collaborative way. Rather than imposing ideas or solutions, the supervisor would share some ideas about the problem, its causes, and possible solutions and next steps (and the reasoning behind each of these) and then invite the employee to share thoughts and the supporting reasoning behind these thoughts. Together they create a shared understanding of where the employee's performance is and, based upon this shared understanding, work collaboratively to determine the next steps.

Even without a title or authority, an employee has the ability to be a my-way unilateralist during or following a performance review. He could unilaterally decide whether to do something, withhold information from the supervisor, or implement the solutions that he thinks best regardless of the supervisor's perspective. Someone doesn't necessarily need to have positional power to be unilateral. But, as with all unilateralist behaviors, both the short- and long-term consequences are counterproductive: the relationship between the supervisor and employee suffers due to the lack of trust, transparency, and agreement, and the employee's performance is likely to remain stagnant or decline because the two aren't working together to find a way forward. Utilizing the collaborative mindset, however, would lead to the employee setting aside the unilateral approach and, instead, working side-by-side with his supervisor to mutually decide how to move forward. The benefit of this collaborative approach is that the supervisor will be right there by the employee's side, fully committed to supporting the employee's future performance success in whatever way has been agreed upon.

See the Parts; Understand the Whole

By casting a wide net and gathering all valid information in a given situation we can better appreciate all of the pieces to the puzzle that make up the situation we are facing. When we understand both the whole context that surrounds the situation and the situation itself, we are more able to make an informed choice about what we need to do next. Collaborators strive to understand both the parts (the specific things that we are focused on) as well as the larger context and the fabric of the whole. Those who subscribe to the collaborative mindset understand the fact that people are moved to make decisions and take actions in their lives based upon the pieces as well as the whole. By understanding the whole—the context of people's lives—versus just focusing on the parts, collaborators can begin to appreciate why people do what they do. Because the larger context of people's lives is as much responsible for their decisions and actions as a specific event or circumstance, when we step back from the details to see the larger frame, we can begin to see what we need to do to effect change within the system and perhaps within others.

An additional benefit of looking at things holistically is that we tend to be more empathetic and understanding toward others and, therefore, more open to their experience, perspective, insights, and so forth. This by no means lets people off the hook for their bad behaviors. As we discussed during our exploration of the assumption *people are simply trying to do the right thing under the circumstances they face*, trying to understand the context of a person's bad behavior and the reasons behind it doesn't mean the behavior is okay or should continue. Using a collaborative mindset, however, might actually enable you to more easily engage people who are doing undesirable things and influence them to do things differently.

When it comes to performance management, there is often a tendency by supervisors and managers to focus on the behaviors of the individual performer and not fully recognize that the employee is part of a larger system that supports or undermines the employee's performance. The late W. Edwards Deming wrote about the 85/15 rule by which 85 percent of an individual performer's outcomes are due to the larger system, and only 15 percent result from the employee's efforts. While people might differ on whether Deming got the percentages right or if he was giving people too much room to dodge responsibility for a performance problem, most of us would agree that the systems always play some part in an individual's performance. That system might include the presence or absence of clear goals, adequate skills training, ongoing feedback, access to essential information resources, cooperation among team members, and a healthy relationship between the supervisor and the employee—to name only a few of the system elements that profoundly affect an individual's performance.

The implications of the 85/15 rule and the importance of looking at the context of an employee's performance, not just the effects of her performance, are that we need to look for *cause* not blame. In performance reviews, my-way unilateralists—in hot pursuit of solutions to performance problems—will often turn to blame rather than cause, focusing their energy on fixing the individual without looking at the context within which the individual works. Unilateralists are rightly looking for solutions to get an employee's performance to where it needs to be. But by looking only at the part and not understanding the whole, the unilateralist might well miss the larger issue that's contributing to the employee's performance problem.

On the other hand, supervisors using a collaborative mindset don't ignore the employee's contribution to a performance problem, but they don't ignore the role of the larger system within which the employee performs either. During the performance review a supervisor using this enacting behavior will not only explore the array of potential causes of a performance problem that include the whats and whys of the employee's specific behaviors but also examine the adequacy of training, feedback, cooperation from others, clarity of expectations, frequency of interaction between the employee and the supervisor, availability of the right tools, and so forth. Supervisors who enact the collaborative mindset hold employees accountable for their performance outcomes, and they also explore other possible causes when things go wrong rather than starting with blame. That's the secret for turning mediocre or adequate performers into stars: believing in their potential, not rushing to judgment about their struggles, understanding the root causes of performance problems, and working collaboratively to find solutions and strategies to leverage employees' talents into great results.

Use Critical Reflection to Examine Deeply Held Beliefs and Behavioral Patterns

The last of our enacting behaviors involves the collaborator looking deeply into the mirror and asking, "What am I thinking or not thinking, believing or not believing, perceiving or not perceiving, doing or not doing that might be limiting my insight and learning—or contributing to the employee's performance problem?" Whereas my-way unilateralists rarely look into the mirror to examine their own contribution to any situation (e.g., "It can't be me. I'm right about this. It's others who are getting this wrong!"), those who follow the collaborative mindset understand that their own fingerprints are all over the murder weapon.

Critical reflection is the capacity to think deliberately about something in such a way that we surface our underlying beliefs, values, and assumptions. Once these beliefs, values, and assumptions are more evident to us, there is a greater possibility that we'll be open to challenging and even changing them when these beliefs, values, and assumptions take us in directions that undermine our relationships and our goals. Critical reflection also includes examining any situation in which we might be struggling and asking how our behaviors are contributing to the situation. Whether the situation involves working relationships between an employee and a supervisor or relationships within our families, collaborators see in such situations that the problem is never just about the other person's behavior. They understand that there is always shared responsibility between the parties. Collaborators understand that the problem is not just that our teenager won't listen, our employee keeps missing performance targets, our coworker isn't focused on details, or our significant other has unrealistic expectations. They recognize that, in each of these relationships, their hand was involved to some degree in steering the relationships along the path it's currently following— and that they can have a hand in steering the relationship in the *right* direction toward a healthier, happier place.

The Greek philosopher Socrates, when faced with the choice between death and banishment from the social discourse of Greek society, chose death. He argued that being cut off from lively dialogue among his intellectual peers was worse than death. As reported by Plato, Socrates declared that "an unexamined life is not worth living" and chose death.[1] Fortunately, most of us aren't presented with a choice as stark as the one that Socrates faced. Most of us have the ability to engage in critical reflection at any time and, with the help of the collaborative mindset, can translate the insights from these reflections into better outcomes in our lives.

Collaborators thrive on examining their lives—on exploring how their own beliefs and behavioral patterns influence their relationships, personal and professional outcomes, satisfaction levels, and so forth. And, once aware of their influence and power, they entertain and explore alternative beliefs and behaviors that may be more facilitative of understanding, learning, and personal growth for themselves and others.

Within the performance review this enacting behavior would involve both supervisors and employees examining their performance partnerships and the employees' performance outcomes and asking some probing questions: How are my thinking patterns, beliefs, and behaviors helping to cause the situation that we're facing? Have I prejudged the other person? Do I believe that the other person is working toward positive outcomes for me and for both of us? What part am I playing in the performance outcomes that we're examining? What are my contributions to the problem, and what might my contribution to the solution look like? What beliefs, assumptions, or behaviors might I need to change to facilitate a better relationship between us and a better performance outcome for both of us?

Unilateralists generally have a hard time asking these questions. And when they do ask them, they have an even harder time answering the questions objectively and seeing how what they're thinking or doing might have contributed to the problem. Collaborators ask these questions routinely and intuitively—and that's what enables them to be great supervisors and star performers.

* * *

Whew! We've covered a lot of ground as we've taken a deep dive into the values, assumptions, and enacting behaviors of the collaborative mindset. And we hope that by now you get the idea that this mindset and particularly the enacting behaviors that we've introduced have the potential for transforming all of our relationships, not just those related to navigating performance reviews.

CHAPTER

WHERE IT ALL LEADS

If you can learn a simple trick, Scout, you'll get along a lot better with all kinds of folks. You never really understand a person until you consider things from his point of view, until you climb inside of his skin and walk around in it.
—Atticus Finch in *To Kill a Mockingbird* (1962)
by Harper Lee

Let's return to Figure 2.2 and quickly review how values, assumptions, and enacting behaviors work in concert to create the outcomes and consequences at the very top of the my-way mindset model. The values drive the assumptions, and together they emerge as a suite of enacting behaviors that lead to a set of outcomes that are profoundly different from those of the collaborative mindset depicted in Figure 5.1. With the my-way mindset's unilateral approach there is a continuing and rapid decline in communication, understanding, problem solving, learning, and effectiveness. Despite (and actually because of) the enacting behaviors of my-way thinking and action, relationships go from bad to worse.

If and when a my-way unilateralist makes the journey toward collaboration, the outcomes begin moving in the opposite direction: there is better communication and understanding, the root causes of problems and challenges are explored and identified, relationships become stronger and healthier, trust between the parties rises, there is less interpersonal conflict (although there may actually be an increase in healthy disagreement and dialogue), more compassion is evident (especially when there is disagreement), people are producing better results, there are deeper and more meaningful conversations about things that matter, and there is collaborative learning.

We think that these positive outcomes are worth pursuing in any relationship, and they are especially worth pursuing when we move into the challenging world of performance management and performance reviews. Considering the sordid history of reviews that we explored in Chapter 1, achieving these outcomes won't be easy. There is much negative momentum to overcome. But with the right values, assumptions, and behaviors, we can make that journey. It's within our reach.

Again, as the poet Rūmī invites us:

Out beyond the ideas of wrong-doing and right-doing, there is a field. I will meet you there.

The Collaborative Mindset and the Performance Review

Let's return to Tom and Brenda's performance review, which we let you vicariously experience in Chapter 1. As we saw, both Tom, the supervisor, and Brenda, the employee, fully embraced the my-way mindset. Both held firmly to their viewpoints, perspectives, and sense of righteousness. As a result, the performance review, even when done under the watchful eye of a third party, did not go well. Tom tried to box Brenda into a corner to get her to accept responsibility for her past performance problems. Brenda presented her list of reasons why the performance problems either weren't problems at all or, if they were, weren't her fault. Using their my-way unilateral thinking and behaviors got them nowhere.

Let's imagine what this review might look like, however, if both adopted the collaborative mindset and approached the discussion and each other with an entirely different set of values, assumptions, and behaviors. We won't get into the actual conversation just yet, including how both Tom and Brenda might structure their interaction to facilitate a more collaborative discussion (that will come in Chapter 16), but it's fair to say that the dialogue between the two of them would be quite different. Here's a glimpse of what it might look like if both Tom and Brenda focused on collaboration instead of my-way unilateralism:

- Tom and Brenda both set aside any assumptions and judgments that they each might have prior to coming together and enter the conversation with a willingness to hear each other's perspective—perhaps for the first time.

- Tom would prepare for the review by first identifying Brenda's strengths and improvement areas and then examining the possible factors and causes—including system causes—leading to her successes and failures.

- Brenda would also prepare for the review by engaging in critical reflection—assessing her own performance successes and challenges and exploring the factors and causes of each.

- When, in advance of the review, Tom identifies a problem with Brenda's performance, he would look in the mirror and identify how his own beliefs, perceptions, assumptions, and behaviors might have contributed to her challenges.

- Tom would complete a draft version of the performance review form prior to the two of them coming together, and he would make it clear to Brenda that it's his goal to hear her thoughts on all of these issues and that he is prepared to make changes to his draft review based upon what she and he learn during their conversation.

- At the beginning of the review Tom would invite Brenda to share her performance self-assessment first so that he could better understand how she sees her work, uninfluenced by his own assessment. Tom explains his reasoning for using this approach (Brenda sharing her assessment first).

- As Brenda talks to Tom about what has been going well and what hasn't been going well with her performance, she would invite Tom to offer his perspective on all of these performance issues.

- When either Brenda or Tom surface an improvement area, they would both turn their attention to the causes that led to the challenges and, based upon these causes, mutually develop ideas and strategies for helping Brenda strengthen her performance in these areas.

- They would listen to each other—especially when disagreements emerge, enabling them to explore the nature of the disagreement to find out how to reach a resolution.

- They would each start with the assumption that the other party would be acting with good intentions throughout.

- There would be no surprises for either Tom or Brenda because nearly all of the issues raised during the review would have been discussed and explored in performance coaching conversations throughout the year.

- Before talking about a specific performance strength or opportunity for improvement, Tom and Brenda would make sure that they were both talking about the same thing. They would agree upon the specifics of the performance issue before talking about causes and next steps.

- There would be no undiscussables between Tom and Brenda. They would both feel comfortable speaking honestly and hearing what the other had to say on any topic relevant to Brenda's performance and Tom's support for her performance success.

- Together they would begin developing a plan for maintaining, strengthening, and improving Brenda's performance and for the ways in which Tom would support her going forward.

Of course Tom and Brenda aren't suddenly going to shift their approach from my-way unilateralism to collaboration; it will take some time for each of them to find their way within this new framework. There will be times when Tom may say the wrong thing (perhaps running with his story or assumption without testing it out) or Brenda might take a defensive posture and avoid responsibility for a problem. If, however, both of them remain committed to this new approach, they'll be forgiving with each other (there's that compassion thing); their relationship can guide both of them toward collaborative problem solving.

Before we delve into specific tools and techniques for translating the collaborative mindset into the ideal partnership for performance between the supervisor and the employee, it might be a good idea to remind ourselves of the larger purpose of the performance review. If we can keep that purpose in mind as we design the best approach to performance management, we'll be in a much better place to achieve our goals for both the review and the larger performance management process.

Let's dig into what performance reviews are all about in the next chapter.

3

What To Do With All You've Learned

Parts 1 and 2 of this book have laid down a critical foundation for understanding why reviews are often fear-inducing and how we can, by embracing a new framework for thinking and acting, move toward truly fearless performance reviews. You've learned about the hazards of the my-way mindset and the governing values, assumptions, and enacting behaviors of its powerful alternative, the collaborative mindset. It's now time to move beyond discussing the mindsets and into the practical ways in which the collaborative mindset can transform the traditional performance review into a coaching conversation.

We'll first examine the purposes of the performance review, introduce a new performance management framework, offer tools for diagnosing performance problems, discuss how to set collaborative performance goals, and prepare for the face-to-face performance coaching conversation. It's in this section, Part 3, where you integrate all that you've learned into a roadmap for your own fearless reviews. You'll strengthen your confidence in your ability to navigating these conversations and gain the tools to help you and your employee to find the route to better, great, or even star-level performance.

10

THE PURPOSE OF PERFORMANCE REVIEWS

> *I haven't got the slightest idea of how to change people, but I keep a long list of prospective candidates just in case I should ever figure it out.*
> —David Sedaris, American humorist and author

Confusion over the *purpose* of the performance review is often where things begin to go wrong. If we're not clear about what we're trying to accomplish during a performance review, then the results will be worse than muddled—we may end up diminishing our performance partnership with the employee, resulting in deterioration in communication, confidence, trust, and, eventually, performance itself.

Traditionally, performance reviews focus on an employee's past performance. They provide an opportunity for managers to present their assessments or appraisals of their employee's work over a defined performance period—typically a year. The core purpose of this traditional performance appraisal is to judge the quality and effectiveness of the employee's contribution to the organization and often to the team, coworkers, and customers as well. This retrospective judgment of the performer's contribution often involves rating the employee on a narrow range of performance dimensions, leading up to an overall rating of the employee's performance.

When well designed, each of these performance dimensions links back to the organization's goals or core values, the employee's job description, activities related to department or team goals, or specific performance improvement goals identified in the previous year's performance review. In addition, a well-designed appraisal system provides feedback to the performer, using specific and measurable performance dimensions. Each dimension is described in both behavioral and outcome terms to give the performer useful feedback on what was expected and how well he met those expectations. On the other hand, poorly designed appraisal systems and their supporting forms tend to define these performance dimensions in overly broad terms (e.g., team player) that often result in an overall rating that is imprecise and subjective.

For the overall performance rating, the better review processes use a Likert-type rating scale, with a set of clearly defined behavioral anchors (e.g., *fails to meet expectations*—does not follow accepted safety standards; *meets expectations*—routinely follows safety standards and demonstrates good safety practices; and *exceeds expectations*—goes above and beyond standard safety practices and frequently offers suggestions for improving safety for self and others). Although the actual scale used may be made up of three, five, or ten options, the end result, regardless of the scale, is often a comprehensive rendering of judgment as to the employee's performance in each core performance dimension and, at the end, his overall performance effectiveness.

The results of the employee's performance review are intended to drive actions at both the employee level for developmental purposes and at the administrative level for larger, organizational purposes. It's crucial that we understand these diverse needs when we design the best review process.

Administrative and Organizational Outcomes

Administratively, there are a number of objectives that the traditional performance review is trying to satisfy at the team, work unit, department, division, and organization-wide levels. Knowing these in advance can help you create a review process that meets these requirements while also meeting the developmental purposes.

- Establish performance goals and measures that will be used for evaluating success in meeting desired performance outcomes.

- Align employee performance with the organization's vision, strategy, values, and goals.

- Differentiate levels of the employee's performance fairly and objectively.

- Identify the knowledge, skills, and abilities required of a performer to achieve desired performance outcomes—which allows us to plan our training and development priorities at the team, work unit, department, division, and organization-wide levels.

- Ensure that the performer is in the "right seat" on the bus. Is this position a good fit for the employee's skills, knowledge, interests and passions, and motivation?

- Identify system barriers to employee performance such as the lack of a good training program, the inadequacy of the information system to give people status reports on quality or productivity, or the absence of well-defined corporate or division goals to give people guidance in their own goal setting.

- Link compensation, rewards, and incentives to performance.

- Use performance-based rationales for layoffs and downsizing.

- Align job descriptions with changing and emerging circumstances and expectations within and outside of the organization.

- Document the employee's performance gaps that support discipline up to and including termination.

- Diagnose (understand the root causes of) employee performance problems.

- Achieve value-added performance results that benefit the organization and its customers, investors, and other stakeholders.

Each of these purposes might be used by a variety of organizational players.

Human resources might use the review for such actions as salary increases (if any), determining the employee's career advancement potential, developing or strengthening the organization's training and development program, and flagging the employee for possible coaching and assistance if warranted. In some circumstances, a sufficiently negative review might form the basis for progressive discipline, leading up to and including termination.

Executives and division or department managers might use the review process for such actions as ensuring alignment with organizational or division strategy and goals, making sure that the right people are in the right jobs, shifting people's job descriptions and performance expectations in response to emerging issues, holding people accountable for meeting division or work unit goals, ensuring that there is a fair and objective process for differentiating employee talent and contributions, making sure that the right behaviors and outcomes are rewarded, identifying training and development needs for the division or department, and identifying and addressing system barriers to employee performance.

Developmental and Employee Outcomes

It's often the developmental needs that are the key drivers for traditional performance reviews. In this area the objectives for the review mostly focus on developing individual employees in order to enhance their performance outcomes:

- Provide performance feedback to the employee.
- Assess employee's performance-related skill and knowledge strengths and areas for improvement.
- Identify employee career goals in relation to current and future jobs within the company.
- Drive performance improvement planning.
- Identify on- and off-the-job training and development strategies to address opportunities for improvement or career planning.
- Identify and document the employee's potential for promotion or advancement.
- Motivate the employee to reach higher levels of performance.
- Establish and strengthen a performance coaching partnership between the employee and her manager.
- Strengthen employee job ownership and self-management.
- Create meaningful outcomes for the organization, customers, and coworkers.

In a well-designed review process, the results from the performance review are used primarily by the supervisor or manager for defining the performance outcomes and goals for the upcoming performance period—again, typically one year in duration. This future-oriented performance planning process should reflect continuing or new organizational and team priorities and outcomes, identify emerging issues and challenges, and spell out an improvement plan to address any performance deficits identified during the performance review. The improvement plan may also identify specific performance improvement goals and define the desired employee behaviors that will help achieve these goals. Finally, this future-oriented plan identifies the steps the supervisor and the organization will take to support the employee's performance. This might include a development strategy that involves training, mentoring, coaching, stretch projects, and other activities to assist the employee in reaching the goals spelled out in the plan. The overarching developmental goal for this forward-looking review is to guide and support the employee in becoming or remaining a star performer.

As you see, organizations certainly expect a lot out of the performance review. When reviews are managed well and participants are using the collaborative mindset, the results are likely to help both the individual and the organization grow and improve. But if they are not managed well or if either or both parties are using the my-way mindset, then the results will frustrate everyone, fear may arise, and individual and organizational goals won't likely be realized.

A Shift in Focus: From the Past to the Future

As we said at the beginning of this chapter, the performance review has traditionally been oriented toward the past and largely focused on evaluation and correction. Unfortunately, both this backward focus and emphasis on evaluation have contributed to some of the fear-inducing aspects of the review that we highlighted in Chapter 1.

Although this traditional approach to the review can still play a positive role in providing feedback to the employee, guiding the development of a performance improvement plan, and influencing key human resource decision making, too often these positive aspects are diluted by this looking-backward focus on evaluation that informs how the review is conducted. The *how* is all-important here because, as we explored in great depth in Chapters 2 through 9, the mindsets of both parties and the nature of their interactions are likely to determine the success of the performance review.

Let's apply the collaborative mindset to the purpose of the traditional performance review and see if we can use the mindset to reframe the review from its historically evaluative and too often unilateral focus toward a new approach—an approach we call the *performance coaching conversation*. This new approach fully embraces the values, assumptions, and enacting behaviors of the collaborative mindset to

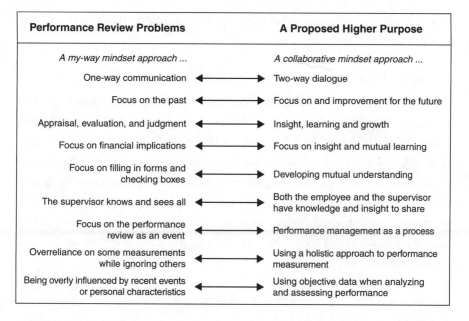

Performance Review Problems	A Proposed Higher Purpose
A my-way mindset approach ...	*A collaborative mindset approach ...*
One-way communication	Two-way dialogue
Focus on the past	Focus on and improvement for the future
Appraisal, evaluation, and judgment	Insight, learning and growth
Focus on financial implications	Focus on insight and mutual learning
Focus on filling in forms and checking boxes	Developing mutual understanding
The supervisor knows and sees all	Both the employee and the supervisor have knowledge and insight to share
Focus on the performance review as an event	Performance management as a process
Overreliance on some measurements while ignoring others	Using a holistic approach to performance measurement
Being overly influenced by recent events or personal characteristics	Using objective data when analyzing and assessing performance

FIGURE 10.1 A Higher Purpose for Performance Reviews

transform the traditional review into something quite different in both focus and structure. We will look at the focus of this new approach in this chapter and save the structure of the performance coaching conversation for Chapter 16. Figure 10.1 highlights common challenges of reviews that are oriented toward the my-way mindset and offers a proposed higher purpose more aligned with the collaborative mindset and integrated into the performance coaching conversation.

Two-Way Dialogue Versus One-Way Communication

The traditional review is hampered in its effectiveness because it tends to focus on what the supervisor has to say to the employee rather than on developing a true dialogue. The limitation of one-way communication is that the supervisor may need to listen more than talk in order to discover the best way to assist the employee toward great performance. It's only through the two-way dialogue of the collaborative performance coaching conversation that mutual understanding and learning occur.

Focus on Improvement for the Future Versus the Past

The performance review, by definition, looks backward at the employee's past performance. Although a historical assessment is a good place to begin, looking only at the past fails to build a foundation for future performance. In a performance coaching conversation oriented toward learning and growth by both the employee and the supervisor, the supervisor uses a historical assessment only as a stepping stone for exploring ways to strengthen performance for the future. This shift in focus moves from a problem orientation toward an improvement orientation.

Insight, Learning, and Growth Versus Appraisal, Evaluation, and Judgment

When the focus is purely evaluation and appraisal (the supervisor rendering a judgment on the employee's work), the review is likely to be more unilateralist in nature (a firm belief in the rightness of one's own position, denial of responsibility, blaming others, and so forth). This response is understandable when you consider what's at stake: an entire year of the person's work history being reduced to a single checkbox on a five-point scale! The resulting defensiveness is a major barrier to communication, dialogue, understanding, and learning during the review. When the employee gets defensive, denies, blames, shuts down, or runs for cover, the supervisor's goal of better understanding the causes of performance difficulties becomes elusive.

If, however, the focus of the performance coaching conversation shifts away from judgment and toward insight, learning, and growth, defensiveness is more likely to fall by the wayside, as both the supervisor and employee work shoulder to shoulder to examine the range of causes of the performance problem and explore ideas for addressing these causes.

Focus on Insight and Mutual Learning Versus Financial Implications

If the higher purpose of the performance review is to facilitate understanding leading to performance improvement, then everything that the supervisor says and does in the review should focus on that purpose. Unfortunately, there's nothing like linking the performance rating of an employee to the resulting pay raise (or lack thereof) to shift the review's focus away from understanding and communication. When there are fiscal consequences for an employee related to which box is checked on the review form, the conversation suddenly shifts to the supervisor defending the evaluation and the employee arguing for a more favorable rating with a more favorable financial implication.

As we discussed earlier, there is a legitimate organizational purpose for linking each employee's performance outcomes with financial consequences. It's worth celebrating great performance and rewarding star performers, and it's also crucial not to reward people who don't hit their agreed-upon targets. The challenge is that the review's focus on financial implications often becomes a distraction from exploring insights and facilitating learning by both parties through collaboration.

We think that it is possible for the supervisor to link the employee's performance review with pay without jeopardizing insight and collaborative learning. The solution rests on how this linkage is made and when this discussion occurs. By simply separating the performance coaching conversation from a discussion of the employee's overall performance rating and its pay-related implications by at least a day, much of the financial distractions can be avoided and the coaching conversation can stay focused on insight and learning. This doesn't entirely rid us of this potential distracter (the employee may rightly assume that the result of this coaching conversation will lead to a box being checked, which, in turn, may have pay-related implications), but by building in some distance between the coaching conversation and the final rating and its pay implications, the space that's created provides an opportunity for meaningful conversation, insight, and learning.

Focus on Developing Mutual Understanding Versus Filling in Forms and Checking Boxes

Nothing that occurs during the performance coaching conversation should interfere with the overarching goal of developing understanding between the supervisor and the employee. Too often, however, the form that's designed to document the review actually becomes a major barrier to communication and understanding. When the focus of the performance review shifts to what's on the form or which box is checked rather than on meaningful dialogue between the supervisor and employee, we believe that the form needs to be temporarily put aside. While the form may still need to be completed by the supervisor and reviewed with the employee, we recommend that the form be viewed as a draft set of discussion points with the final assessment and checkboxes completed *following* the performance coaching conversation. Seeing the review form as a draft also helps ensure that the supervisor is open to learning new information during the coaching conversation, and it lets the employee know that the assessment isn't set in stone—that it's still possible to influence the supervisor's assessment.

A post–coaching conversation completion step for the review form ensures that the final written document submitted to human resources reflects the best thinking by the supervisor, informed by an open and meaningful dialogue with the employee, leading to insight and collaborative learning. Once the form is completed, a brief follow-up meeting with the employee can be scheduled to discuss the final document, the overall rating, and any pay-related consequences.

Both Employee and Supervisor Have Knowledge and Insight to Share Versus the Manager Knows and Sees All

One of the biggest mistakes supervisors can make as they prepare for and conduct performance reviews is to assume that what they see or understand about employees' performance represents all of the facts. This my-way mindset is a problem because when supervisors' perceptions are assumed to be the only facts that count, there is little room left for employees to offer their own perspective. As we learned in Part 2 where we explored the collaborative mindset, the supervisor has a perspective on the employee's performance and the factors influencing it, but so too does the employee—and the employee's perspective is just as important to surface and discuss as the supervisor's. Understanding and honoring each other's perspective is, as we hope you've learned from this book, one of the key underlying assumptions of the collaborative mindset and should be one of the key assumptions of the fearless performance coaching conversation.

When the supervisor and employee agree, the coaching conversation shifts to building on this common ground to develop consensus regarding next steps. When either the supervisor or employee has knowledge or insight that the other doesn't have, however, the coaching conversation needs to shift to identifying, understanding, and honoring these differences—and then using the insights from this dialogue to find a way forward. Both parties in this performance partnership have important information, knowledge, and insight to share. The higher purpose of the performance coaching conversation that's focused on collaborative learning is to mine these diverse perspectives as the two parties work toward the goal of strengthening their partnership and improving the employee's performance.

Focus on Performance Management as a Process Versus the Performance Review as an Event

The performance review or performance coaching conversation is certainly an event, but if this event is viewed in isolation outside of the larger framework of ongoing, continuous performance management, then its full benefits will never be realized. An employee achieving great performance doesn't happen by accident, and it certainly doesn't happen because of one performance coaching conversation each year. When the supervisor and the employee see the performance coaching conversation as a culmination of the many "check-in" conversations that they have had throughout the year, then this annual summary conversation takes on its proper role and function—and there is likely to be fewer surprises and less fear. Viewing performance management as a process anchored to a performance partnership between the employee and the supervisor and seeing the performance coaching conversation as a final integrating step of this process help ensure that the supervisor and employee focus on performance every day of the year.

Using a Holistic Approach Versus an Overreliance on Some Measurements While Ignoring Others

It's easy to document the duration and number of calls an employee makes at a call center; it's harder to measure the quality of these interactions. This is one of the major challenges of traditional performance reviews: too often they focus on things that are easy to measure but might not be meaningful, and they don't focus enough on the things that matter most because their measurement can be difficult. Measuring performance success is one of the key goals of performance reviews in which the employee and supervisor look back on performance expectations defined early in the year and then determine if and to what degree these expectations were met.

The traditional review tends to over-rely on data that are the easiest to gather—such as the number of times something was done, the frequency with which the employee's outputs met certain specifications, and the conversion ratio between attempts and results (e.g., closed deals compared to total sales calls made). A performance coaching conversation informed by the collaborative mindset takes a more holistic approach to measurement. At the beginning of the performance period, the employee and supervisor mutually agree upon the employee's performance expectations and also agree upon ways to measure if and to what extent the employee achieved or moved closer to these outcomes. This discussion should include both the easier-to-measure quantitative data, such as numbers, frequencies, and completion rates, and

qualitative data such as the *quality* of the interactions with customers, the *quality* of the information being communicated by the
employee, and the *quality* of the written reports. Developing clear
measures of these qualitative aspects of employees' work can be
difficult, but it is essential to do if coaching conversations are to
accurately and objectively capture and assess whether employees
have accomplished their performance outcomes. Employees will
find it harder to become star performers if they don't know what a
star looks like!

To paraphrase the British mathematician and physicist Lord
Kelvin, "If you can't measure it, you can't manage it!"[1] The challenge for both the employee and supervisor is to figure out a way to
measure performance dimensions and outcomes that contribute the
most to star performance. Once there is agreement regarding these
more powerful and holistic measures of performance, the dialogue
during the coaching conversation about the measures that matter is
more likely to translate into insight and learning around actionable
information that the employee and supervisor can use to help drive
the employee's future growth and performance.

Using Objective Data When Analyzing and Assessing Performance Versus Being Overly Influenced by Recent Events or Personal Characteristics

Our final problem with traditional performance reviews has more
to do with psychology than with the nature of the performance
conversation. There are two psychological characteristics that are
especially problematic during performance reviews or even performance coaching conversations. The first, called the *recency effect*,
finds that people are cognitively biased toward recent stimuli or
observations and away from earlier stimuli or observations. This
means that, during performance reviews or coaching conversations,
a supervisor who is unaware of this effect might focus on events
that happened last week or last month rather than on events at
the beginning of the performance period. Regardless of whether

the recent event was a positive or negative one, the event tends to loom larger in the supervisor's mind and would therefore tend to be given greater weight. The recency effect is defeated by the collaborative mindset, which cultivates a broad back-and-forth flow of information between the supervisor and the employee and a strong performance partnership that is the result of the employee and supervisor having met to discuss performance on a regular basis. Within this framework, the annual or summative performance coaching conversation is just the last of a series of coaching conversations that have occurred throughout the year where performance successes and challenges have been discussed and explored. The recency effect can also be overcome by the employee and supervisor taking steps to document the employee's performance throughout the year and then integrating that documentation into the performance coaching conversation.

Another psychological characteristic that often gets in the way of an effective review is the *halo-horn effect*. In this situation, people are cognitively biased to view a single dimension of an employee's performance, such as interacting well with customers or coworkers, as representative of the employee's performance in all other areas. In other words, when an employee does one thing very well, the resulting angelic halo causes the supervisor to not see problem areas. The flip side is the horn effect. In this case, when an employee does something wrong, such as missing a mission-critical deadline, the resulting devil's horn causes the supervisor to not see areas where the employee might actually be performing well.[2]

For either of these psychological tendencies, the antidote is for the supervisor to again develop a strong performance partnership with the employee, develop mutual agreement with the employee regarding the multiple measures of successful performance, use objective data when analyzing and assessing performance, document positive and negative performance events when they occur throughout the year, and have numerous performance conversations throughout the performance period.

From Performance Reviews to Performance Coaching Conversations

We've examined the variety of purposes for the performance review and explored how to fulfill these purposes while expanding the review beyond its traditional confines. We also identified the role that the collaborative mindset plays in helping both the supervisor and the employee reframe the review from a backward-looking evaluation of the employee's performance to a forward-looking performance coaching conversation that is focused on insight, collaborative learning, growth, and achieving star-level performance.

Our goal in writing this book is to help you create or contribute to a fearless performance coaching conversation. To get you to that place we have a few more stones to turn over. One of these stones is putting the fearless review—or, rather, the performance coaching conversation—into the larger context of the partnership for performance between the supervisor and the employee. Another is redefining performance outcomes and expectations from good enough to great. These are the first steps for moving all employees to star-performer status: setting a very high bar for performance expectations and building a strong performance partnership. Let's examine what great performance looks like and explore the key ingredients of a strong partnership for performance.

11

ESTABLISHING A FRAMEWORK

> *If you don't know where you are going, any road will get you there.*
>
> —Lewis Carroll, English author

When you buy a book called *Fearless Performance Reviews*, it's a pretty good bet that you're looking for a book on how to prepare for, structure, and navigate the performance review. We think that we would be doing you a disservice, however, if we delivered only on that promise and didn't anchor the performance review or performance coaching conversation within a larger framework—an overarching approach to performance management.

The larger context of performance management needs to be discussed because the event of the performance coaching conversation is really just that: an event within a larger performance partnership between the employee and the supervisor and the employee and the organization. To ensure that your coaching conversations are fearless and actually contribute to employees becoming star performers, you will need to understand this larger framework.

What You Need to Understand About Performance Review

Performance Reviews Aren't that Important

In the great scheme of things, performance reviews aren't that important.

Okay, we admit that we've overstated this a bit. But we're trying to make an important point: providing specific feedback on and appraising the quality of someone's performance *are* important to helping create star performers, but these events are only pieces of a much larger performance management framework. In reality, performance reviews are no more important than any of the other elements of this approach.

"What do you mean?" we can hear you saying. "The performance review is no more important than the other elements of performance management?!" And our response is, "Yes, absolutely." While organizations tend to place extraordinary importance on reviews (as noted in Chapter 10), we need to see that the other elements within the performance management system are assigned equal importance. Based upon some of the ideas in this book you might develop a truly great performance-review methodology to guide yourself and others in conducting successful reviews, but if you don't understand or haven't mastered all of the other components that contribute to star-level results, then even your performance coaching conversations are likely to come up short. If you take the time to strengthen every aspect of performance management, not just the coaching conversation, you increase the chances that great outcomes will be achieved at every level.

Let's take a look at this larger framework within which the performance coaching conversation takes place. Figure 11.1 depicts this framework and gives it a name: the *great performance management cycle.* We'll spend some time discussing this cycle because it is the foundation for everything that needs to happen throughout the entire performance process and profoundly influences what happens during the

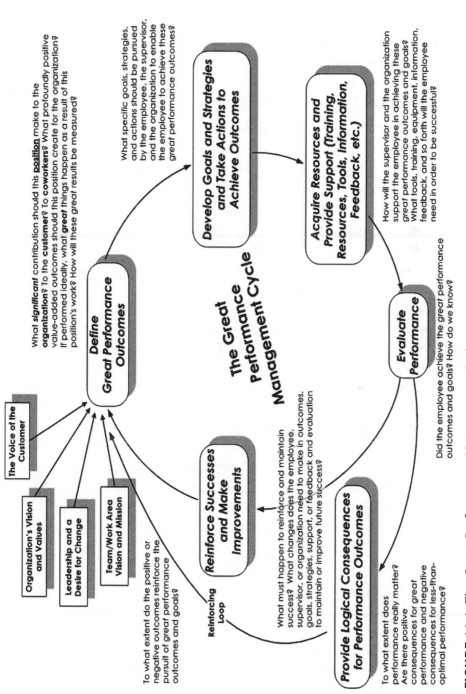

FIGURE 11.1 The Great Performance Management Cycle

performance coaching conversation. And if the entire process is managed well, you're likely to see very little fear and significant insight, learning, and growth.

Define Great Performance Outcomes

It's at the top of the great performance management (GPM) cycle where performance management begins and where the *purpose* or *aim* of the employee's work is defined. The word *great* is used here intentionally. The purpose should be defined in such a way that the outcomes or results of the employee's efforts make a significant and profoundly positive contribution to the organization. We use the word *great* to help elevate this purpose to the highest level—to ensure that when we conceive of the aim of an employee's contribution, our thinking moves far beyond ordinary, just-get-by performance.[1] In this first step of the GPM cycle, our goal is to define the extraordinary outcomes for a position such that these become the driving target of the employee's efforts. By helping the employee imagine what great performance outcomes for his position actually look like, the employee is more likely to create these positive results and move his performance to the star level.

We like to think of great performance in terms of three types of profoundly positive outcomes: outcomes that uplift and serve the customer or client at the highest level, outcomes that contribute to and strengthen the team and coworkers, and outcomes that strengthen and help grow the organization as a whole. Figure 11.2 offers an example of a great performance outcome for a department manager.

Within the established great performance outcomes for the organization, customers, and team, there are five crucial dimensions of great performance that the employee needs to address for each outcome area: *quality, quantity, cost, timeliness,* and *impact on others*. These additional layers of expectations provide further insight into what great performance might look like and help focus the employee's efforts toward achieving truly great results in each of these areas.

Customers	Team	Organization
As a result of the manager's work, the department's customers' needs are consistently and reliably exceeded. The manager anticipates customer needs, expectations, difficulties, challenges, and opportunities and then channels the effort of others in the department to achieve extraordinary results that routinely surprise the customer. The manager achieves these great performance outcomes for customers by building a strong partnership with customers, which involves listening to, displaying empathy for, and proactively responding to emerging customer needs. The manager is accessible. Customers feel comfortable approaching the manager at any time when quality, productivity, or timeliness problems arise. The manager continually seeks out ways to exceed expectations through routine dialogue sessions where emerging issues are explored and the partnership is strengthened.	As a result of the manager's work, department team members consistently exceed their performance expectations, they are highly engaged in work that they find meaningful, and they bring their full talents in service to customers, the team, and the company. The manager achieves these great performance outcomes for team members by building a strong coaching relationship with direct reports, setting high expectations for all, holding frontline supervisors accountable for team member growth and development, and actively encouraging taking personal responsibility and job ownership. The manager is open, empathetic, and focused on mutual learning while, at the same time, sets high standards for performance and accountability. The manager listens more than speaks and sees disagreements as opportunities for finding creative solutions to department challenges.	As a result of the manager's work, the department goes above and beyond the strategic expectations set for it by the organization. The organization is, as a result, financially and programmatically stronger, more effective, more efficient, and more responsive to changes both within and outside of the organization. Other departments look to this department to lead the way in terms of best practices for talent management, innovation, process improvement, and so forth. The manager achieves these great performance outcomes for the organization by paying close attention to emerging issues both within and outside of the organization, asking questions that reflect strategic thinking and insight, constructively challenging conventional wisdom, sharing best practices, paying attention to efficiencies and cost control, and contributing to other departments' successes by actively exploring ways to help them achieve their goals.

FIGURE 11.2 Great Performance Outcomes: Department Manager

How might a supervisor and an employee determine what the great performance outcome expectations should be? As displayed in Figure 11.1, these profoundly positive outcome expectations naturally reveal themselves when we ask customers what matters most to them; when the performance outcome implications from the organization's vision are clearly articulated for each position; when leaders, managers, and supervisors have a clear vision of the desired performance outcome expectations for a position—which might take the position in an entirely new direction (hence the reference to change); and when the vision or mission of the employee's department, work area, or team suggests specific outcome expectations.

A critical next step in defining great performance for a position is the articulation and integration of these specific performance outcomes within the position or job description. Because the position description is the keystone for defining everything that is expected of an employee, the great performance outcome expectations must be spelled out in this document. If an employee will be held accountable for achieving great performance, then the position description needs to reflect these expectations. Unfortunately, position descriptions too often focus on describing behaviors and activities or offer general outcome statements about the role and function of a position. While behaviors, activities, and general statements about the position's role are important, by themselves they are not sufficient for providing performers the clear and compelling performance outcome direction that employees need.

By spelling out in the job description the specific great performance outcome expectations that result from all of the job behaviors and activities, the larger purpose of the employee's work becomes much clearer. To provide greater clarity of purpose and to ensure that employees focus on what matters most to customers, coworkers, and the organization as a whole, it is essential that position descriptions be written in ways that reflect these great performance outcome expectations.

Note how the example in Figure 11.2 typically focuses on the results of the employee's work rather than on the processes, behaviors, or activities used to achieve those results. While processes, behaviors, and activities are obviously important in getting to these great results, for the first step of the GPM cycle it is critical to focus primarily on outcomes rather than on *how* the employee is to achieve these results.

This step of the GPM cycle also involves identifying how performance results will be measured. For the greatest positive effect on performance, every great performance outcome should have an agreed-upon performance measure that enables both the employee and the supervisor to know if and when the outcome has been successfully achieved. Lacking a method of measurement, both the employee and the supervisor may have a hard time gauging whether the outcome has been achieved. Working from the collaborative mindset, the supervisor and employee mutually define outcome metrics at the beginning of the GPM cycle; this reinforces the idea of accountability for these outcomes and establishes a built-in feedback process that is essential later on in the cycle.

Develop Process Goals and Strategies

In the first step of the GPM cycle the goal was to have the supervisor and employee agree upon and develop a clearly defined vision of the great performance outcomes that becomes the aim or purpose of the employee's efforts. The second step in the cycle involves defining specific *process* goals, strategies, actions, and behaviors that the employee, supervisor, and others will need to take to ensure that these great performance outcomes are achieved.

Whereas the great performance outcomes focus on results, the goals, strategies, actions, and behaviors that are defined in this second stage of the cycle tend to deal more with processes—the "hows" of either maintaining the employee's current great performance or moving the employee from her current performance level closer to great performance.

These hows might involve the employee setting goals such as:

- Improving work processes or procedures
- Increasing individual effectiveness by pursuing training and development in specific competencies
- Reducing error rates or problems with quality
- Building stronger partnerships with customers
- Strengthening working relationships with peers
- Taking the initiative at improving the safety record of the team
- Being more innovative in work methods and processes.

These hows might also involve the supervisor or the organization setting goals such as:

- Consistently having team-level discussions about great performance so everyone is on the same page in terms of desired outcomes and their progress in getting there
- Upgrading the customer relationship–management system to align closely with the organization's definition of great performance
- Implementing an organization-wide six-sigma program to improve quality and productivity
- Consistently sharing customer feedback with teams and individuals
- Creating an intranet site to facilitate employees sharing best practices
- Holding monthly "vision-and-values" meetings of employees to help translate the abstract vision and values into everyday behaviors and practices

The process goals, strategies, and actions identified in this step of the GPM cycle should include any goals, activities, and behaviors that will help move the employee toward achieving great performance. Each of these goals, strategies, actions, and so forth should be measurable such that both the employee and the supervisor will know if and when each has been achieved or if improvement is desired.

As with defining great performance outcomes, these process goals, methods, and behaviors must be firmly anchored in the employee's job description. The job description should be reviewed at least annually to ensure that it accurately spells out both the great performance outcomes and the position's essential job functions that collectively move the employee toward these outcomes. Because these essential job functions are the backbone of each employee's performance, every expectation, goal, strategy, and behavior outlined in the second step of the GPM cycle must be linked back to these functions.

Ensure Organizational Support

With the employee pointed in the right direction—toward great performance outcomes and working with a set of process goals, strategies, and actions—the next step in the cycle comes into play. Acquiring or providing organizational support involves the employee and the supervisor identifying, acquiring, and delivering the information, training, tools, resources, and other forms of support that employees require to translate their efforts into great performance.

In this step of the GPM cycle the employee, his supervisor, and the organization work together to ensure that there is an infrastructure that focuses on supporting the employee in achieving the desired performance results. For the employee this means taking the initiative to identify what resources he will need to get the job done and then being assertive about acquiring these resources. For the supervisor this means taking steps to ensure that, to the greatest extent possible, the resources identified by the supervisor or employee are made available to the employee.

This supportive infrastructure is always specific to each employee and the great performance outcomes she is expected to achieve. Some broad areas of organizational support identified by the employee or supervisor might include such things as:

- Providing the employee opportunities for skill and knowledge development and training
- Ensuring the employee's access to critical job-related information
- Ensuring that the employee has the tools and equipment needed to be successful in the job
- Identifying and removing system barriers and obstacles to performance (e.g., poor information system, uncooperative peers in other departments, and tensions between team members)
- Ensuring frequent employee-supervisor communication and interaction

- Ensuring frequent updates on emerging issues and challenges affecting the employee's efforts or results

- Updating the employee on emerging issues within the company, industry, market, and so forth that might have a bearing on his performance

- Sharing specific customer and team member feedback with the employee

- Providing opportunities for the employee to work on special projects that might interest her

- Facilitating or mediating the resolution of disagreements between the employee and others (e.g., customers, coworkers, and peers in other departments)

- Providing ongoing feedback to the employee on his performance

Providing organizational support is a central contributor to great performance because it enables the employee's effort toward the desired results. When the supervisor and organization provide this supportive infrastructure, there is an increased likelihood that the great performance outcomes will be achieved. Doing so also lets the employee know that the supervisor and the entire organization want to see her become or remain successful. And while some people can become star performers in the absence of such support, when the support systems are present, the path to great success will be faster and far more likely.

Evaluate Performance

The next step within the GPM cycle—evaluate performance—is the step that we usually focus on whenever someone raises the topic of performance management. As we discussed earlier in this chapter, however, the actual review is only a single step within this larger performance management framework, and, ideally, this step should occur more than just once during the year. Evaluate performance is the time when the employee and supervisor each reflect upon the original per-formance target (the great performance outcomes and the supporting suite of goals and behaviors) and then compare it with actual results achieved.

With skillful guidance from supervisors during performance coaching conversations, employees explore their performance results and the likely causes of these positive or less-than-optimal outcomes. We'll dig deeper into the performance coaching conversation later in this book, but, for now, we want to make the point that the success of this step of the GPM cycle depends upon everything that pre-ceded it:

- A clear and compelling list of great performance outcomes
- A supportive set of goals, strategies, actions, and behaviors to help the employee achieve these outcomes
- A strong organizational infrastructure that provides the support that the employee needs to achieve the great performance outcomes and goals

With these elements in place, the performance evaluation is simply the natural next step as both the employee and supervisor keep their watchful eyes on the desired great performance outcomes and goals, assess the extent to which the employee's actual perfor-mance moves closer to these outcomes and goals, and then begin to explore opportunities to maintain, strengthen, and improve the employee's efforts toward achieving these desired results.

Reinforce Successes and Make Improvements for the Future

The final step of the GPM cycle extends the dialogue that began during the evaluation phase by identifying and exploring opportuni-ties where employees can maintain and reinforce their strengths and strengthen areas where performance improvement is needed. In this step of the process, the employee and the supervisor mutually iden-tify a set of actions that each can take to build upon, maintain, and reinforce the employee's past success and shore up areas where the employee's performance can be improved.

Here are some examples of actions that the employee and supervisor might take to maintain and reinforce success and strengthen and improve employee performance:

- Clarifying, adjusting, strengthening, or modifying the great performance outcomes in such a way that they may be clearer, more easily measured, easier to attain, and so forth
- Adjusting and modifying existing *process goals and strategies*—or adding new ones that reflect improvement areas or new work priorities
- Identifying new ways in which the supervisor or the larger organization can provide organizational support—or adjusting the level of support provided in the past to reflect new priorities, challenges, or constraints
- Changing the nature, focus, frequency, or structure of the *evaluate performance* step of the process—including refining the review to strengthen the dialogue and the relationships between the employee and supervisor
- Shifting the employee's work priorities to reflect new initiatives or emerging issues
- Adding new responsibilities that reflect the organization's strategic priorities
- The employee enrolling in a skill- or knowledge-development course to address perceived skill or knowledge gaps
- The employee taking steps to strengthen relationships with customers and strategic partners

It is in this critical final step of the process where insight and learning emerge from the dialogue that began during the evaluate performance step. And when this phase of the cycle is informed by the collaborative mindset, the insight and learning flow with ease, as both the employee and the supervisor explore these issues together and then mutually decide upon an improvement strategy and plan. The *performance maintenance, growth, and improvement plan* is developed at the end of this phase with a focus on moving the employee's performance toward his great performance outcomes in the next iteration of the cycle.

The *reinforce success and make improvements* step is the final step in the GPM cycle. There remains one additional component of our performance management framework that acts as an additional reinforcing loop to ensure that the employee's energy, passion, and activities remain focused on her great performance outcomes: providing logical consequences for performance outcomes.

Provide Logical Consequences for Performance Outcomes

It's fair to say that, in general, people aren't like Pavlovian dogs who salivate on cue, waiting for a juicy steak to suddenly appear after hearing a bell. People's responses to various stimuli (positive rewards or negative consequences) always involve some measure of decision making and choice. It's important to note, however, that people do pay attention to the positive or negative consequences they experience based upon their behaviors or results. Whether the organization actively manages it or not, both the planned and unplanned consequences that employees experience based upon their performance outcomes have a profound effect on their future behavior.

When an employee experiences positive consequences or rewards that soon follow actions that move her performance outcomes closer to great performance, then these positive rewards tend to encourage behaviors that keep the positive rewards coming. If an employee experiences negative consequences following performance that misses the great performance target—or moves further away from this target—then these negative consequences tend to encourage behaviors intended to prevent these negative consequences. The purpose of providing positive or negative consequences for performance results is to reinforce the desired behaviors and outcomes and discourage behaviors and outcomes that run contrary to great performance. Figure 11.3 offers several examples of positive and negative consequences that might influence employee behaviors and results.

Supervisors who want their employees to engage in the right behaviors and achieve desirable results and discontinue the undesired behaviors and results need to take this reinforcing loop within the cycle seriously. This involves the supervisor directly providing clear and meaningful consequences (both positive and negative) for performance. It also involves the supervisor being aware of less formal positive or negative consequences coming from others that may also be influencing the employee's behavior and outcomes. Other players who might be providing positive or negative consequences include coworkers and customers, other teams with whom

Example Positive Consequences	Example Negative Consequences
• A financial reward or bonus	• Loss of autonomy and independence
• Advancement opportunity	• Withdrawal of an opportunity for a financial reward or bonus
• Greater independence and autonomy	
• A letter of commendation	• A corrective action letter or memo documenting the need for the performer to improve performance
• A simple "thank you" for the employee's contributions	• Reduction in flexible work schedule opportunities
• Flexible work schedule	
• Ability to work from home	• Withdrawal of opportunities to work on high-visibility or -status projects
• Opportunity for high-visibility or -status project assignments	• Disciplinary letter
	• Demotion to a lower-status or lower-pay position
• Modifying the job in ways that are aligned with the employee's passions and interests	
• Opportunity to take a lead role on a project	• A simple expression of disappointment by the supervisor
	• Taking away job responsibilities that the employee may enjoy most

FIGURE 11.3 Example Positive and Negative Consequences for Performance Outcomes

the employee interacts, the larger organizational culture (e.g., the informal values and beliefs that work with or sometimes against the desired outcomes such as, "We don't encourage people to pursue outstanding performance. It makes it harder for everyone else."), or even the employee's family and friends. Unfortunately, these other positive or negative consequences—which may work as cross purposes to the great performance outcomes and goals—often fly under the radar and outside the supervisor's awareness. When peers celebrate an employee's success, that's a wonderful informal reinforcement to keep doing great work. When a cynical veteran of the organization mumbles to the employee that he shouldn't work so hard because the organization will never recognize his efforts, the supervisor's efforts to encourage hard work may be significantly undermined.

Unfortunately, supervisors often have little control over many of these other reinforcers. They should, however, at least be aware of them in order to either leverage and further reinforce the positive forces in the environment or to offset or counterbalance the negative consequences that might work against what they are attempting to accomplish when working with employees.

A key factor in *providing logical consequences* as part of the GPM cycle is that the employee needs to see the natural connection between her own behaviors and outcomes and the positive or negative consequences that she receives as a result. The employee must see that great things naturally follow after doing the right behaviors and achieving the desired outcomes and that less-than-desirable consequences follow the wrong behaviors and outcomes.

Who's in Charge of the Great Performance Management Cycle?

We've spent a good deal of time walking you through the GPM cycle and have identified a set of activities that need to occur at each step of the process if truly great performance is to occur. One question we haven't yet answered, however, is this: Who is in charge of this process?

When we ask this question in our workshops, the answer is almost always "the supervisor!" This is understandable. When it comes to actually managing the performance of an employee, it seems that this would fall to the supervisor. After all, the supervisor is the one the organization looks to when an employee fails to contribute in the expected way. In reality, the person who is most responsible for moving along the GPM cycle is the employee. Each employee is always fully responsible and accountable for his own performance—good or bad. While the supervisor must take an active role in guiding the employee through the GPM cycle, at the end of the day it is the employee—working closely with the supervisor—who needs to define the outcomes, set the goals, identify and acquire the resources needed to accomplish the outcomes and goals, evaluate whether the target has been met, and identify opportunities for maintaining success and improving where the results didn't meet expectations. Within the GPM cycle, the supervisor fulfills the role of a coach—guiding, shaping, challenging, questioning, provoking, supporting, encouraging, and inspiring the employee to take on the challenge of achieving great performance. As in the sports arena or the performance stage, however, the supervisor as coach generally doesn't walk onto the field or step onto the stage. This is the purview of the employee. Defining expectations, doing the job well, engaging in the right behaviors, gathering performance data, self-assessing and correcting performance as necessary, and so forth are all the responsibility of the person who is actually doing the work. When it comes down to setting and achieving the goal, it is up to the individual athletes, musicians, actors, or employees to make it happen; the coach is there just to help the person along on the journey.

The Partnership for Performance: The Employee and the Supervisor Working Together

While the employee is primarily responsible for her performance and the resulting outcomes, the supervisor as coach still plays a critical role. Together, the manager and employee forge a partnership for performance that is focused on guiding and supporting the employee toward achieving the established great performance outcomes. Who actually takes the lead within this partnership at any given time, however, is a function of the skill, knowledge, and experience of the employee—with the coach responding with the correct amount of direction, guidance, support, feedback, and reinforcement.

Figure 11.4 highlights the nature of this dynamic partnership for performance. As shown in this figure, early on in the partnership the supervisor (depending upon the skill, knowledge, and experience level of the performer) may initially take the lead role in defining performance outcomes, establishing goals, identifying supportive resources, providing feedback on performance, and suggesting improvement goals. The coach may also take this more assertive role when the employee is having performance problems. Even at this end of the relationship, however, the employee remains fully engaged in each of these key steps in the GPM cycle and remains fully responsible for the resulting performance.

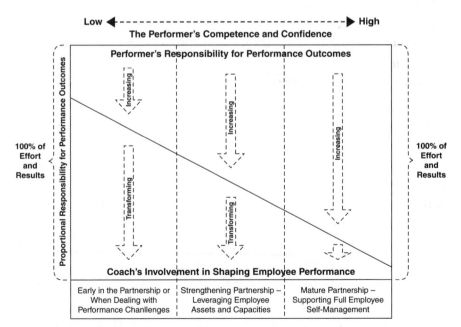

FIGURE 11.4 The Dynamic Partnership for Performance

As the employee gains competence and confidence, however, the supervisor might downshift his own role and focus instead on leveraging the employee's assets and cultivating the employee's capacity to self-manage. This downshift includes moving away from taking the lead in defining great performance, setting goals, identifying resources, and so forth and moving toward guiding the employee into taking full responsibility for these steps. The supervisor and employee work together to determine the best role for the coach based upon an assessment of the competence and confidence of the employee. As the employee's competence and confidence grows, the coach shifts to a more supportive role through skillful dialogue, probing questions, encouragement and suggestions, and constructive feedback. Figure 11.4 displays what this shift in responsibility might look like as both the performer and the coach transition their roles to a redefined version of their performance partnership.

If the employee experiences a setback or if new challenges arise that test the competence and confidence of the employee, the supervisor and employee might mutually decide it's appropriate for the supervisor to step forward and ramp up his level of involvement. Once the employee regains her footing or becomes more competent and confident in her performance or the new challenges or responsibilities, the supervisor's level of involvement can then be scaled back. This dynamic partnership for performance between the employee and supervisor is always in flux as the job changes, challenges rise and fall, and the employee's competence and confidence rises and sometimes falls as well.

Even for star performers, the supervisor as coach never disappears from the scene. While star performers need far less guidance and direction, support, assistance with problem solving, reinforcement, and so forth as compared to employees who are struggling, the supervisor still stays engaged at some level. Star performers need supervisors to challenge them, encourage them, give them feedback, suggest new directions, and reinforce that they are on the right track and that others are paying attention to their results.

Some organizations adopt the philosophy that supervisors should focus all of their attention on encouraging and supporting the star performers and simply get rid of the marginal ones. In most cases, however, the stars don't really need lots of care and feeding. We also think that it would be a mistake (and quite unilateral, in fact) to write off the marginal or poor performers prematurely. When dealing with a marginal or poor performer, supervisors should instead adopt the collaborative mindset—set aside their assumptions and judgments, gather valid information, explore the context of the employee's work, look for the underlying causes, and so forth—to find out what the supervisor or the employee might be missing that explains the performance gap between expectations and actual results. If we do discover what's missing, we just might find the magic that helps transform this marginal performer into a good performer and, if we're lucky, even a star player. And where would we be if we had unilaterally rushed to judgment and pushed the employee out the door? Our own work results would likely have suffered as we covered the duties of the vacant position while simultaneously recruiting and hiring someone to fill the position—and, if we're lucky to find a match, start the process all over again.

The GPM cycle offers supervisors and employees a powerful framework for defining expectations, identifying needed resources and support, evaluating results, and translating this evaluation into insight and learning to maintain or improve future performance. The partnership that these two players forge early on within the GPM cycle and the expectations that they have for each other throughout this cycle largely determine the employee's success in achieving great performance. The GPM cycle provides a roadmap for navigating this performance partnership in a way that leads to greater employee engagement and better results. And it increases the likelihood that the employee can become a star performer—because a vision of what great performance looks like is defined and the employee knows that it's up to him to make that happen. Employees are responsible for their success. No one else can make great things happen—not the supervisor, not coworkers, not the department, and not the organization.

DIAGNOSING WHY THINGS GO RIGHT OR WRONG

> *Do not condemn the judgment of another because it differs from your own. You may both be wrong.*
>
> —Anonymous

S tar performers are easy. They tend to be self-starters, they don't need a lot of our attention, they frequently solve problems before we're even aware of them, and they don't drain us of emotional energy. Imagine what it would be like if all the employees on our team were star players ... our organization wouldn't likely need us!

Unfortunately, not all of our employees are star players. While a few employees consistently achieve and even exceed great performance outcomes, and a large majority does a decent job of meeting expectations, there is almost always a small subset of employees who struggle at achieving their performance goals. The upside of this diversity of performance success is some degree of job security for people in supervision! The downside is that it's sometimes difficult to determine the factors that cause some to soar, others to get by, and still others to have difficulty with minimally achieving their basic performance expectations.

The solution to understanding these factors involves exploring causation. Behind every star player, every employee who just gets by, and every employee who struggles with making the grade, there is a cause. If we can understand the causes driving performance success or failure, then the path to great performance becomes much easier. And, within the context of a performance coaching conversation, we can focus our efforts on leveraging the success factors while understanding and addressing the factors that may be undermining employee performance.

What's Behind a Star Performer's Success?

It's fair to say that when an employee consistently exceeds expectations and goes above and beyond what others doing comparable work are achieving, something different is clearly going on for this employee. A star employee's success is usually due to a combination of factors. These might include the employee's internal motivators and success drivers; the employee's relationship with her supervisor; the employee's belief system that includes a sense of personal responsibility, accountability, resilience, and resourcefulness; and a supportive performance environment (including having sufficient resources, cooperative team members, access to information, and effective feedback systems).

For employees who are performing at the star level, the supervisor's task is to recognize, celebrate, and reward their extraordinary performance to ensure that it continues. This requires both the employee and the supervisor to explore the forces that are enabling the employee's success. To ensure continued star-level performance, the causes of great performance should be defined, reinforced, and amplified during the performance coaching conversation and throughout the performance period. Once the employee and supervisor determine the "recipe" for success for the employee, then both need to take actions to ensure that these success factors remain in place to support future levels of extraordinary performance.

We believe that anyone has the potential to become a star performer. The trick is to find out what will engage each employee to move his performance to a new level. So, as we diagnose what enables star-level success in order to sustain it, it's also useful to think of ways to replicate these factors so that all employees might experience a boost in performance.

Here are some of the key performance drivers of star players.

Star Players Don't Get There Alone

All great basketball players—those who consistently score the most points during a season—clearly don't become star players on their own. To make a basket you need the ball, and to get the ball one of your team members has to pass it to you at the perfect time and at the perfect speed. And even after the star player gets the ball the team continues to take actions that support that player's goal of sinking the ball in the basket. The same forces are in effect for our organization's star players. While they may bring extraordinary insight, skill, resourcefulness, and resilience to their work that enables them to soar past conventional performance expectations, they achieve their success in concert with the help of others. The support that these stars get from others might involve sharing crucial information, offering technical advice, helping to problem solve, offering encouragement, providing feedback on ideas, and removing performance barriers. In all cases, star performers are not alone; they achieve these performance outcomes because of the assistance and support of others.

Personal Initiative and Responsibility Matter

Star players often achieve great results because they see opportunities that others may not see and then step forward to seize these opportunities. While personal initiative may be a deeply embedded aspect of someone's personality, it's crucial that supervisors reinforce and support this characteristic when it surfaces in the star employee. Supervisors should also communicate personal initiative as a core expectation of great performance for all employees, not just those performing at the highest level.

Related to personal initiative is personal responsibility—where employees see themselves as responsible for their own success. Star performers tend to fully embrace this philosophy and feel that their own actions determine their success trajectory. As we discussed in the last chapter in respect to the great performance management cycle, this should be an expectation for all employees. When employees feel responsible for their own success, they tend to have greater ownership of their work, display greater personal initiative, and take a more active role in working through and around performance obstacles. They generally don't let system barriers or obstacles stand in the way of their performance success.

Creativity, Innovation, and Risk Taking

Star performers tend to achieve their performance goals by thinking creatively, being innovative, taking risks, and being bold. They are successful in large part because they are unconventional—they color outside the lines, and they look for innovative ways to achieve extraordinary results. To sustain great performance in these star performers supervisors again need to expect, celebrate, reinforce, and reward such audacity. While audacity and risk taking may need to be tempered by reasonable boundaries or parameters, if supervisors want to ensure that their best performers continue to turn in extraordinary performance, then these qualities need to be encouraged.

As with the other suggestions we've offered in this area, expecting, celebrating, and reinforcing creativity and risk taking should apply to the entire workforce, not just the star performers. While the my-way mindset might suggest that most employees can't be trusted to take acceptable risks or act audaciously, the collaborative mindset encourages us to challenge this assumption and judgment and firmly believe that all employees have the ability—to varying degrees—to rise up to such expectations and to do so in ways that are likely to surprise us (in a good way!).

The Supervisor Functions as a Coach

As we have discussed in Chapter 11, moving people toward great performance requires that a supervisor adopt more of a coaching role. In this coaching role the supervisor identifies the best set of supporting, guiding, directing, and correcting behaviors needed to enable an employee to achieve her best. For a star performer this means determining the best role to play. Does she need my encouragement and support? Does he need occasional feedback? Does she need someone to bounce ideas off of? Does he need to be challenged?

In every case—for a star performer or a potential star performer (which should be just about anyone on the team)—the supervisor should ask the employee, "What do you need from me to achieve great performance? What do you need from me to help sustain your success?" And, if the employee-supervisor dialogue is informed by the collaborative mindset, then the answers that emerge are likely to help sustain a star performer or enhance the effectiveness of one with star-level potential.

During a fearless review, star performers don't need much direction and feedback from their supervisor. What they might need instead is a fresh challenge, a new stretch goal, or an exciting assignment that rekindles their creative energy. And potential star performers may need a show of support or confidence from the supervisor, assistance with problem solving, feedback that says, "You're on the right path!," or whatever else the rising star performer might indicate that he needs from his coach.

A Supervisor's Expectations Can Be Self-Fulfilling

As we discovered in our exploration of mindsets and their influence upon how we see and interpret the world, the my-way mindset often leads us to focus on information that is consistent with our beliefs about people while ignoring information that doesn't agree with our beliefs, assumptions, and judgments. The effect of this narrowing of information is that we tend to see only the things that we want to and not see the things that we don't want to. This comes into play for star performers as well as potential star performers in that our expectations for others tend to be self-fulfilling.

This tendency is called the Pygmalion effect. The effect is named after Pygmalion, a Cypriot goldsmith and sculptor in Ovid's *Metamorphoses*—a story in Greek mythology. In the story, Pygmalion falls in love with a female statue that he has carved out of ivory and, because he loves the statue and wishes it to become real, the statue comes alive. The basic premise of this effect is that our expectations tend to be self-fulfilling; we get what we expect to get. The Pygmalion effect was demonstrated in the classroom in a famous study by Robert Rosenthal and Lenore Jacobson,[1] where they found that a teacher's positive or negative expectations of a student influenced the student's academic performance. The research found that this effect often occurred below the radar: teachers unconsciously behaved in ways that facilitated and encouraged the students' success or failure.

In the workplace this effect can manifest through a supervisor's internal beliefs and prediction of the employee's likely success or failure. This prediction can then, directly or indirectly, come true. The supervisor expects to see a star performer and is only aware of star-performer behaviors and outcomes, or (in the opposite direction) the supervisor expects to see a poor performer and is only aware of poor-performer behaviors and outcomes. In either of these situations, the supervisor's observations tend to reinforce her belief that someone is indeed a star or poor performer.

Why should we care about this effect when considering how to reinforce and sustain a star performer's success? Just increasing our awareness of how our expectations influence our perceptions can tune us into the subtle and not-so-subtle ways in which we might reinforce a star performer's effectiveness—and how our expectations can also contribute to poor performance in those we don't believe will succeed:

- Giving a star performer greater freedom to define his job in ways that maximize his talents, passions, and contributions while perhaps limiting such freedom to those who haven't "earned" it

- Giving the star performer a high-profile assignment (and not giving it to others) and expecting her to shine

- Seeing only the upside of the employee's performance (e.g., commendations from the CEO) while not noticing the downsides (e.g., complaints from other team members about the employee not sharing the credit for the great outcomes)

- Taking the time to listen to the employee's ideas and strategies for achieving great results—and not taking the time to listen to the ideas of those whom we don't believe are on the track to exceeding expectations

- Viewing a star performer's failures as learning opportunities that will enhance his future success while perceiving the failures of a mediocre performer as true to form and consistent with our expectations that this person isn't working out

Level of Job Engagement

The research is in: employees who are fully engaged with their work tend to bring far more energy, commitment, drive, and creativity to the task. When we strengthen employee engagement, we are likely to see performance by all employees—star performers and potential star performers—taking off. While there are a variety of employee engagement models being used by organizations today, we view the following as some of the more important factors that contribute to high engagement and, subsequently, high performance[2]:

- Job design and enrichment—employees are actively involved in designing the outcomes, processes, and parameters of their jobs; their work is personally meaningful; there is a good match between the job requirements and each employee's talents and abilities; and the employee's talents are fully utilized.

- Fair treatment and equity—employees feel that they are treated fairly in terms of recognition, rewards, and job and career advancement opportunities

- Sense of community—employees feel connected to a community where others care about them as individuals, value and recognize their ideas and contributions, and support them when they are challenged or experience setbacks

- Strategic alignment—employee energy and effort are directed at performance results that directly affect the bottom line: high-quality outcomes, lower costs, higher productivity, and higher customer satisfaction

- Organizational support—employees have the skills and knowledge that they need to do their jobs, are given an adequate transition time for learning new tasks, have adequate staffing levels in their work areas to achieve their performance goals, are encouraged to grow and develop professionally, and have access to the resources, tools, technology, and equipment that they need to do their jobs well

- Personal strength and resilience—employees feel confident in their own abilities to meet almost any performance challenge, are comfortable with change, believe that their efforts are driven by a clear purpose or vision, and feel responsible for their own success

Star performers tend to be very engaged because, in general, they believe that much of the work that they are doing is within their sphere of influence, they have the support they need from others and the organization, they feel that what they do matters (or they would be less likely to do it as well), they feel fairly treated and recognized by the organization, and they feel a part of something larger than themselves. Supervisors can help sustain a star performer's engagement levels by paying attention to and ensuring that these engagement factors remain in place.

For potential star performers a supervisor should examine what engagement elements are in place and ensure that they stay in place. The supervisor should also identify engagement dimensions that are not in place and then work with the employee to strengthen those engagement levels.

When we are preparing for a fearless performance coaching conversation, we need to spend as much time exploring the causes of success as we do exploring the factors that are potentially undermining it. As we have highlighted in this chapter, performance success has a number of potential causes. A fearless review must involve the supervisor and the employee exploring together the origins of what's going right—and then ensuring that these factors are reinforced and sustained as the employee moves into the next performance cycle.

Exploring Common Barriers to Performance Success

Every traditional performance review, even fearless ones, focuses at least part of its time identifying gaps between expectations and actual results and exploring opportunities for closing these gaps. While sometimes these gaps are major performance challenges for an employee, other times they are simply a reflection of a desire by the employee and supervisor to move good performance to an even higher level. Gaps, therefore, aren't necessarily negative; they represent opportunities for improving or enhancing an employee's performance outcomes.

Regardless of the type of gap between expectations and actual performance, however, the causes behind the gap need to be explored in order for the employee to experience an improvement in this area in the next performance cycle. For this reason, exploring causation is a crucial step in improvement planning. Whether this planning occurs before or during the performance coaching conversation, both the employee and supervisor need to consider the factors that may have played a part in the employee's performance coming up somewhat (or significantly) short of expectations.

Here are some of the major causes of performance challenges that employees might encounter—challenges that even star performers might experience as well.

Performance Expectations Weren't Clear

Sometimes employees miss the target because they really weren't sure what the target was. This lack of clarity might emerge simply from the failure of the employee to talk about expectations, with both supervisor and employee making assumptions about what was great, acceptable, or unacceptable performance. At other times this problem may arise when most of the discussion between the employee and supervisor focused on the how of the work rather than the what—the desired outcome. Talking about how to do a job is quite different from describing the end result, and for many jobs the differences between the what and the how are critical. While it is important and sometimes critical to define the how, if, and when of each party's expectations on a specific dimension (especially concerning matters of safety, quality, timeliness, cost, and so forth), in general most of the focus while setting performance expectations should be on the what—the outcomes of the employee's work.

Is it possible or desirable for an employee to begin a performance cycle without clear expectations? Sometimes it may actually be appropriate for an employee to begin a task with an agreed-upon ambiguity in outcome expectations. Perhaps the employee is tackling a new project or task, and she is charting new territory. It's okay if the employee and supervisor agree up front that neither is quite sure what success at the task might look like. In this situation the key to assessing the success of a new project is that as the employee moves closer to achieving the emerging outcome, she is routinely checking in with the supervisor to provide updates. This verifies that the employee is still heading in the right direction and making appropriate adjustments in behaviors. What we don't want to see is the employee marching down a specific path that she defines without consulting her supervisor and the supervisor eventually being surprised with the outcome at the end of the process. When beginning a task with an ambiguous outcome, both the employee and the supervisor need to stay in contact as the outcome begins to emerge from the employee's work.

Finally, even if the expectations are clear, the metrics of success may not be. Both the employee and the supervisor need to agree upon what is expected not only in terms of performance but also in how success will be measured throughout and at the end of the cycle.

Here are some questions to explore at the beginning of and throughout the performance cycle to ensure that this challenge doesn't become a barrier to the employee's performance: How does the employee define success on this performance dimension? How does the supervisor do this? To what extent are either of these definitions malleable as the employee's performance moves forward? What measures of success will be used to evaluate whether these expectations have been met? Does the supervisor have expectations for the how as well as the what? If so, does having the employee focus some attention on the how matter in a meaningful way when gauging the employee's performance?

The Employee Hasn't Received Performance Feedback Throughout the Year

As we learned early on in this book, a fearless review is characterized as having no surprises. For the employee this involves the employee and supervisor having frequent performance coaching conversations throughout the performance period. As we'll learn in Chapter 16, these periodic performance coaching conversations should be relatively informal and unstructured with a focus on both parties just touching base with each other, checking in on the employee's progress, discussing challenges, and, in general, discussing what's going well and what's not going well.

If both the employee and the supervisor are too busy to have these coaching conversations and the interactions between them are infrequent, then there is a greater chance that there will be surprises—in either direction. Yes, with all of today's information technology tools there are a variety of non-face-to-face ways for employees and supervisors to stay connected and for the supervisor to be made aware of the employee's performance progress. While there is really no good substitute for regular in-person performance check-ins, if necessary, these can be done via the phone or web conference. In the absence of frequent check-ins—even with automatically generated performance metrics reports delivered to the supervisor—it will be much harder for the supervisor to really know how things are going and to provide ongoing feedback and support to the employee. And, in the absence of frequent check-ins, the employee might continue further along a path that's headed in the wrong direction. With more frequent feedback from her supervisor, this problem is far less likely.

Here are some questions to explore at the beginning of and throughout the performance cycle to ensure that this challenge doesn't become a barrier to the employee's performance: How often should we get together to check in on the employee's performance throughout the year? In what way and how often will the supervisor receive data on the employee's performance outcomes? How would the employee prefer to receive performance feedback throughout the year (e.g., face to face, phone, e-mail, or web conference)? How would the supervisor prefer to give performance feedback throughout the year (e.g., face to face, phone, e-mail, or web conference)? Note: on these last two questions, it isn't just for the employee or supervisor to unilaterally decide how these sessions will occur and when. While it's important to discuss the employee's and supervisor's preferences, it's up to the two of them to mutually decide upon a check-in and feedback process that works for both of them. That's the collaborative mindset way!

The Great Performance Expectations Were Too Challenging or Unrealistic

The performance cycle starts off with audacious expectations to help ratchet up the employee's performance. Perhaps these bold performance outcomes were suggested by the employee, who wanted to demonstrate his commitment to achieving these results. Or perhaps the supervisor felt that it was time to challenge the employee to perform at a much higher level and urged the setting of these stretch expectations. Regardless of what led to the high expectations, it's now the end of the cycle and performance came out below expectations. One driver of this gap between great expectations and actual results is that either the employee, supervisor, or both had an unrealistic idea of what the employee could accomplish. This might have been due to incorrect assumptions about the employee's competence and confidence levels or an incorrect reading of what this higher performance expectation might require from the employee or the organization.

Another possible driver of this gap is that while the employee may have the competencies and confidence to meet these high performance expectations, such issues as other workload pressures, inadequate tools or resources, and lack of support from others may erode the employee's ability to meet expectations.

If the supervisor and employee had had frequent coaching conversations throughout the performance period, they would have had a chance to do performance check-ins and, once they both realized that the bold performance expectations weren't likely to be achieved, the outcomes could have been revised to a more realistic level—or the employee and supervisor could have devised a learning and development plan to address any employee skill or knowledge requirements to suit the performance expectations.

Unfortunately, if this cause of the performance gap is only discovered at the end of the cycle, it's too late to scale back expectations or ramp up the employee's skill or knowledge development. That's why the employee and the supervisor need to have frequent coaching conversations throughout the year to ensure that the expectations and competencies of the employee are aligned and then make adjustments in either or both if not.

Here are some questions to explore at the beginning of and throughout the performance cycle to ensure that this challenge doesn't become a barrier to the employee's performance: Do the employee and the supervisor have a good sense of the employee's competence and confidence levels? Are the high performance or stretch expectations reasonable given the employee's skills, knowledge, and self-confidence level? Is the employee's workload reasonable given these expectations? Do these expectations cause the person to stretch her capabilities in the right way? What additional skill or knowledge development might help the employee achieve these expectations?

The Employee Doesn't Have the Skills, Knowledge, Ability, or Experience to Do the Job

This cause of performance gaps, similar to the last cause, is less about audacious expectations that are beyond the employee's reach and much more about the employee simply not having the basic skills, knowledge, ability, and experience to achieve the outcomes and goals. Perhaps there has been a poor match between the person and his job—suggesting that the hiring process might have been flawed. Or perhaps the employee has the skills and knowledge but not the experience of translating these skills and knowledge into quality results. Regardless of the origin of this cause, when the basic skills, knowledge, ability, and experience aren't present in the employee, performance is likely to suffer.

Addressing this problem involves a more thorough analysis of the job and the skills, knowledge, ability, and experience required to do the job and an assessment of whether the employee has the right mix of talent, ability, and experience. If not, the solution might involve shifting the employee into a job with a better fit, investing in more skill or knowledge training, assigning a mentor or coach to guide the employee's experience development, or exposing the employee to lower-risk challenges to develop his skills and experience.

Here are some questions to explore at the beginning of and throughout the performance cycle to ensure that this challenge doesn't become a barrier to an employee's performance: What are the skills, knowledge, abilities, and experience required of an employee for success in this job? Does the employee doing this job now have these competencies and capacities? Has the job changed such that new skills and knowledge are required? Has the job outgrown the employee? What experience could this employee be exposed to early on to help her achieve these performance expectations? Who might best mentor or coach this employee to enable him to develop the right skills, knowledge, and experience for these performance expectations?

Inadequate Access to the Tools, Equipment, Resources, People, and Information Needed to Achieve Expectations

It's hard for employees to hit targets if they don't have the right tools or information in hand. Achieving performance expectations depends upon an alignment of an employee's skills, knowledge, ability, experience, and motivation with the proper tools and access to crucial job-related data.

Tools and equipment might include computer hardware and software, hand tools, safety equipment, and clothing.

Information resources might include instructional manuals and reference materials; quality, productivity, and scrap reports; run charts; test results; and access to Internet and company intranet sites.

People resources might include access to subject matter experts, experienced peers, other human experts, and those in positions of influence or power who could support the employee's performance.

When this area is identified as a potential driver of less-than-optimal performance results, both the employee and supervisor need to step back from the employee's daily performance behaviors and ask, what are the tools, equipment, people, and resources that are foundational to the employee's success? And then, based upon the answer, develop a plan to ensure that these resources are made available to the employee when needed. This would involve the employee taking a lead role in acquiring access to some of these resources, while the supervisor might be in a better position to ensure the availability of organizational and system resources.

Here are some questions to explore at the beginning of and throughout the performance cycle to ensure that this challenge doesn't become a barrier to the employee's performance: What are the tools, equipment, information, and people resources that the employee needs to have access to in order to achieve the performance expectations? Who will take the lead role in acquiring these resources? How might the supervisor be most effective as a resource to the employee on an ongoing basis? How should the employee identify new tools, equipment, and resources that might be useful throughout the performance period? If the employee's performance expectations are elevated during the performance period, how and when will the need for additional tools, equipment, and resources be addressed?

Ineffective Relationships with Others and the Presence of Team or Workgroup Conflict

When the team isn't functioning well, when there is tension and discord among employees, and when people spend significant amounts of time protecting themselves from real or perceived threats from others, performance of individuals and the entire team takes a hit. As we learned in our exploration of the my-way mindset, the protective and counterproductive strategies of unilateralism often arise when people feel the need to fend off an attack, avoid embarrassment or blame, and so forth—all of which can occur when people disagree or are in a conflict situation. And when people move into a my-way mindset, they don't share information; they avoid responsibility, they point fingers, and they focus on winning and not losing. The result is that performance deteriorates as people are focused on defending and not on performance quality and productivity.

So when conflict or discord is identified as a potential driver of missed performance targets, the employee and supervisor need to explore the root causes of the tension and develop a plan for addressing the causes. Whether the conflict arises from misunderstanding, past history among the parties, competition for scarce resources, insensitive behaviors, or a lack of empathy and compassion, both the employee and supervisor need to take steps to prevent the discord from further eroding performance.

Here are some questions to explore at the beginning of and throughout the performance cycle to ensure that this challenge doesn't become a barrier to the employee's performance: What is the health of the employee's working relationships with key information providers and collaborators? What actions can the supervisor take to strengthen working relationships within the team and with other teams in the organization? What mechanisms are in place for resolving disagreements and disputes? How confident does the employee feel in dealing with conflict on her own—or is there a role for the supervisor in some conflict situations? What conflicts and tensions might be anticipated that could affect the employee's performance, and what actions can the supervisor and employee take to proactively prevent or reduce these potential conflicts?

Limited Access to the Supervisor

The employee's supervisor always plays a key role in shaping an employee's work life experience and her performance outcomes. As we discussed in Chapter 11, the role of the supervisor as coach is a dynamic one: as the employee's competence and confidence grow, the supervisor's role diminishes; as new challenges arise that push the employee out of his competence and comfort zones, the supervisor can step up the degree of her involvement. Whatever the degree of supervisory involvement in assisting the employee with routine or extraordinary performance challenges, the supervisor never disappears. The role changes, but she always plays a role.

A sustainable partnership for performance between the employee and supervisor depends upon an ongoing conversation throughout the performance period where each party assesses the expectations of and need for each other. The supervisor should always have the capacity to be accessible to the employee to assist with decision making, problem solving, brainstorming, idea sharing, and so forth. A key responsibility of the supervisor as coach is remaining mindful of this dynamic relationship and being prepared to move closer to or away from the employee as the employee's performance and needs suggest.

When the relationship isn't strong and effective, when there is misunderstanding and a lack of trust, when the employee is hesitant to approach the supervisor or the supervisor hesitant to approach the employee, and when there is infrequent communication regarding crucial matters of performance expectations and outcomes, then the employee's performance is likely to be negatively affected. If these conditions are present, then both the supervisor and employee should acknowledge the need to invest in building a stronger relationship. While the employee has an important role to play here and needs to courageously speak up if he feels that the relationship isn't strong, we believe that the supervisor carries the primary burden of ensuring the health of their partnership. If the role of a coach is to do whatever it takes to bring out the best in another, then the coach has to be the first to step forward to ensure that this is happening.

Here are some questions to explore at the beginning of and throughout the performance cycle to ensure that this challenge doesn't become a barrier to the employee's performance: What is the health of the working relationship between the employee and the supervisor? What actions should each take to strengthen communication, understanding, and the relationship as a whole? Does each trust the other to act in his interest? How often should the two of them touch base, share issues, discuss concerns, and so forth? How will the two of them resolve disagreements? To what extent does each bring the collaborative mindset into their everyday relationship? What actions should each of them take to ensure that the enacting behaviors of this mindset define their relationship?

The Absence of Clear and Positive Rewards for Great Performance or Negative Consequences for Mediocre or Poor Performance

As we discussed in Chapter 11, people need to see that there are consequences for performance, good and bad. When employees hit their great performance targets, this needs to be recognized, celebrated, and rewarded. When they miss their targets, this too needs to be noted, discussed, and explored, and fitting consequences for failing to meet performance expectations need to be experienced by the employee. We're not suggesting punishment, rather we are simply talking about making sure that employees know that performance matters—that supervisors and perhaps the entire organization notice when someone achieves good or great performance and when they don't. If performance doesn't matter to the supervisor or the organization, then why should it matter to an individual employee?

Employee motivation is always an internal act. Supervisors, peers, and others in the organization cannot motivate individual employees; employees can only motivate themselves. Supervisors, peers, and others can, however, better understand what an employee's internal motivators are and then do their best to deliver these valued rewards when the employee produces results. But if others and especially the supervisor don't recognize, celebrate, or reward an employee's performance results and instead take the employee's performance for granted, the employee might say to himself, "Why am I working so hard? No one seems to notice or care!"

When no one seems to care about an employee hitting, exceeding, or missing the performance target, results might eventually matter less to the employee as well. Supervisors can help reduce the negative effect of this factor on an employee's desire to meet or exceed expectations by always making sure that the employee knows that performance does matter. The supervisor and employee need to discuss the positive rewards for great performance at the beginning of the performance cycle, and then they both need to work hard to ensure that when the employee achieves great results that these positive rewards follow. And, if the employee misses some or all of the performance targets, the positive rewards don't follow—at least to the same degree as for successful outcomes.

Here are some questions to explore at the beginning of and throughout the performance cycle to ensure that this challenge doesn't become a barrier to the employee's performance: What is the range of positive rewards for great performance available to a successful employee? What rewards does the employee value the most? What are the consequences of the employee failing to achieve the desired performance outcomes? What positive rewards naturally follow when the employee achieves his performance outcomes?

A Disability Is Limiting the Employee's Ability to Achieve the Desired Performance Outcomes

Sometimes when employees fall short of expectations, it's not for the lack of skills, tools, peer or supervisory support, access to information, or internal drive; it may be because there is a physical, mental, or emotional disability. In many cases the disabilities that people have can easily be accommodated, and there is little impairment in job function or outcomes. In other cases the disability may be significant enough that a simple accommodation may not be enough, and the employee's performance may be impaired.

Under the Americans with Disabilities Act (ADA), organizations have a responsibility to be sensitive to employees' disabilities and to provide reasonable accommodation to enable them to perform their job at a level equivalent to those without a disability. The goal of the ADA is to ensure that people with disabilities are able to work and perform with the same rights and freedoms as someone without a disability. For supervisors this means being tuned into the possibility of physical, mental, or emotional disabilities limiting an employee's performance and being ready to explore the need for a reasonable accommodation.

If a supervisor suspects that an employee may have a disability impairing the employee's work behaviors and performance, the first step is to contact human resources to discuss how to initiate a discussion with the employee. Human resources can provide guidance to ensure that the topic is raised sensitively and in compliance with the ADA. If an employee approaches the supervisor, identifies that she has a disability, and requests a reasonable accommodation, the supervisor should first contact human resources to explore the next steps in responding to the employee's request.

In either situation, once a supervisor is aware of the possibility of an employee having a disability, in most cases there is an obligation under the ADA to take action. The goal is not just to meet the letter of the ADA law but, more importantly, to enable an employee to perform at his best and to meet or exceed performance expectations.

Here are some questions to explore at the beginning of and throughout the performance cycle to ensure that this challenge doesn't become a barrier to the employee's performance: Does the employee report that he has a disability that impairs his job performance? Does the supervisor observe the employee struggling to perform specific job functions? Are there patterns in work behaviors or results that suggest a physical, mental, or emotional disability impairing the employee's job performance? Has the employee self-identified himself as having a disability? Has the employee requested a reasonable accommodation?

The Employee Is Experiencing a Personal Problem, Lacks Motivation, or Demonstrates Inflexibility

The last of our major drivers of less-than-optimal performance is the cause that almost exclusively falls within the purview of the individual employee. While the previous causes of performance gaps that we've explored involve a shared responsibility with the supervisor often taking a lead role in addressing the cause, this final obstacle to performance results largely rests with the employee.

If the employee is experiencing a personal problem that's interfering with the job, then it's up to the employee to address this on her own. If the supervisor becomes aware of the employee having a personal problem, he should encourage the employee to contact the company's employee assistance program (EAP). EAPs can be very effective at helping an employee sort out options when dealing with personal challenges and allowing the supervisor to focus exclusively on job performance.

If the employee lacks motivation or inner drive to perform, this too is up to the employee to address. While the supervisor plays an important role by creating an environment that employees might find motivational, it remains the responsibility of each employee to connect her inner drive to the work that she does every day. If employee motivation is the issue, a supervisor can spark a conversation with the employee about what her internal drivers are, what she gets excited about, what she values most about the job, and so forth, but again it's up to the employee to make the connection between the work that she is doing and what she finds inspiring. It may be that what the employee is looking for in terms of rewards or motivating outcomes just isn't possible in the job that he is doing. In this case, "finding their happiness elsewhere" (to paraphrase a famous Disney human resources slogan) may be what needs to happen. The "elsewhere" could be in a different job within the organization, or it might mean that the employee and the organization need to part company. The supervisor may need to initiate this conversation to enable both the employee and supervisor to achieve a shared understanding as to whether there is good alignment between what the employee values most and what's possible in the job.

When the barrier to employee performance is a function of the employee's work style, personality, and behavioral preferences, this too becomes the employee's responsibility to resolve. If the employee is deeply resistant to change, is unorganized and unable or unwilling to create structures to manage work effectively, is unable or unwilling to work collaboratively with others, or is unwilling or unable to accept direction from others, then these become issues of the employee's performance accountability. A supervisor should raise these issues during the performance coaching conversation as part of the larger discussion about the employee's job performance and then work with the employee to develop a plan for resolving these performance issues that might include "finding their happiness elsewhere."

Here are some questions to explore at the beginning of and throughout the performance cycle to ensure that this challenge doesn't become a barrier to the employee's performance: Based upon the employee's work style, personality, and behavioral preferences, what challenges might the employee face as she approaches the new performance period? How will these challenges be overcome such that they don't become barriers to the employee's performance? What are the employee's internal drivers? What excites his passions?

Does the employee appear to be struggling with personal problems? How does the organization's EAP work and how best should the supervisor reference EAP to the employee?

If You Understand Cause, You Can Sustain or Change Just About Anything

If you want people to keep doing something (e.g., sustain their good or great performance), then you need to understand the drivers—the factors that enable, support, and will likely sustain their efforts. And if you want to understand why people aren't doing something at the level you expect or hope for, then you need to understand and address the underlying causes.

This chapter started off by exploring the range of possible factors that may be enabling star performers to become and stay star performers. Supervisors who want to help everyday performers to become star performers and their star performers to stay at the top of their game should make an effort to identify and examine these success factors and then work with employees to cultivate or strengthen these factors in the workplace.

The latter part of this chapter identified a long list of factors that, if not addressed, could undermine an employee's performance. When an employee misses a performance target, any one or a number of these causes may be behind the problem. The first nine of these factors tend to be areas where the cause actually begins with the supervisor's actions or the actions of the larger organization. As a result, supervisors must be proactive in identifying what they are doing or not doing that could be contributing to a performance problem and then addressing these areas if change is warranted. The employee plays a crucial role in surfacing these issues and concerns and engaging the supervisor in addressing such things as setting clearer goals, providing ongoing feedback, and providing training and tools. The supervisor needs to look in the mirror and ask, "What am I doing or not doing that's contributing to this employee's performance challenges?" The purpose of this question is to help supervisors identify how they can be most helpful at getting the employee's performance back on track.

If the supervisor's efforts are informed by the collaborative mindset, then the conversations between the employee and the supervisor are likely to be constructive and productive, leading to a shared understanding of what each needs to do to move performance to the next level.

It's time to integrate the ideas we've explored in this book and focus on preparing for conducting the fearless performance coaching conversation. Before we have this face-to-face conversation between an employee and supervisor, we need a roadmap to ensure that all the key issues have been examined and explored. Chapter 13, Laying Down the Foundation for Success, offers a planning roadmap that leads us deep into preparing for an effective performance coaching conversation.

13

LAYING DOWN THE FOUNDATION FOR SUCCESS

> *"If you don't know where you are going, you will probably end up somewhere else."*
> —Laurence J. Peter, author of *The Peter Principle*

The date for conducting the performance coaching conversation is on the horizon, and it's time that you started pulling your thoughts together. Based upon a reading of this book you've consciously moved away from the fear-inducing my-way mindset and toward the collaborative mindset to ensure that you have the right mental model for understanding the employee's performance level. You have also gained a better understanding of the purpose of the review within the larger context of the great performance management cycle. And finally you have a clearer understanding of the array of possible success factors that enable truly great performance and the factors that might undermine performance.

It's time to bring all of these insights and perspectives together along with your observations of the employee's performance and supporting documentation as you prepare for the face-to-face performance coaching conversation.

Laying down the foundation for success, of course, is something that you do throughout the performance period—not just in the final few days before the performance coaching conversation. Preparing for the conversation starts at the very beginning of your relationship with the employee by establishing clear expectations, continues as you document the good and bad of the employee's performance, and is sustained through the frequent performance conversation check-ins that you have with the employee. Being prepared means that you are constructively engaged in the employee's performance by observing, assessing, discussing, providing feedback, and coaching (e.g., guiding, supporting, directing, teaching) when necessary. If you are engaged throughout the performance period, then doing your preparations for the formal performance conversation is far easier and a lot less fear inducing.

The Steps to Successful Performance Reviews

Reviewing the Employee's Performance Expectations

Planning for a fearless coaching conversation begins by examining the expectations defined at the beginning of the performance period. As we discussed when we introduced the great performance management cycle, the performance expectations for an employee arise from two primary sources: the job description and the great performance expectations discussion that evolved from the previous performance period and that also reflected the organization's priorities and emerging issues. At this point in the process—at the *end* of the process—there should be no surprises. No new performance expectations are introduced by the supervisor. Both the supervisor and the employee are using the same point of reference for the conversation: the outcome expectations established at the beginning of the performance period, which were perhaps adjusted during the period if warranted by new organizational, departmental, team, or individual work priorities.

The job description is a foundational document that represents the official expectations defined by the organization for a position.

When well written, the job description should include a statement of the great performance outcomes for a position as well as a list of five to seven core job responsibilities and the outcome expectations for each of these responsibility areas. This is the starting place for every supervisor and employee when setting performance outcome targets at the beginning of the performance period. It's also when the supervisor and employee first start planning for the performance coaching conversation: What were the official outcome expectations for this position that represent the core responsibilities that the employee was expected to fulfill?

If you've followed the advice in this book, the beginning of each employee's performance period is also when you worked collaboratively with the employee to define what great performance actually looks like and identified an array of outcomes and goals that became the employee's target for the upcoming performance period. In addition, at the beginning of the performance period and based upon the employee's performance in the previous period, you and the employee likely defined a set of outcome and goal expectations that involved maintaining, improving, or growing the employee's performance in specific areas.

So as you prepare for the performance coaching conversation, you gather up the job description, the great performance outcomes and expectations that enact the job description within the performance period, and the specific outcome and goal expectations resulting from the previous review. These are the expectations that you and the employee will use as the key measures for assessing whether the employee met, failed to meet, or exceeded expectations.

This is the first step. The second step involves collecting data on the employee's performance.

Gathering Employee Performance Documentation

As with reviewing the employee performance expectations, the process of performance data collection is something that both the employee and supervisor do beginning on the first day of the performance period.

Because our memories are challenged by the passage of time, it's crucial that both the employee and the supervisor agree upon and develop a methodology for documenting the employee's performance throughout the performance period.

For some jobs—especially those that focus on numbers such as production, sales, and call centers—there is an immediate stream of often automatically generated data that both the employee and the supervisor can use to assess whether the employee is meeting productivity and quality goals. For many jobs, however, there isn't a steady stream of automatically generated performance data that's readily available to the employee and supervisor. In these cases, if the performance coaching conversation is to be objective and data-based, the employee and supervisor need to agree upon the measures of success and then develop a method for collecting and documenting this data.

In addition to system-generated performance data or data that the employee and supervisor might collect throughout the performance period, there are some tools that the supervisor can use to ensure that the review is based upon objective information rather than vague recollections of what might have happened six months ago. These are the performance log, critical incidents log, documentation e-mails, and performance portfolio.

Performance Log

The performance log is an informal record kept by the supervisor that notes significant examples of an employee's accomplishments, behaviors, failures, successes, milestones, setbacks, awards, and so forth. If you use the performance log, it must be used to record positive performance as well as performance problems and should be maintained for all employees—not just for those who may be experiencing problems. The goal of the performance log is to maintain an objective record of the employee's key performance outcomes. The log is not maintained in secret by a supervisor. To the contrary, following the value of transparency within the collaborative mindset, the supervisor readily shares anything written on the log with the employee. In fact, everything that you write down on a performance log is discussed with the employee at the time you document it—nothing hidden, no surprises.

Critical Incidents Log

The critical incidents log approaches documentation similarly to the performance log. The critical incidents log also documents positive performance as well as performance problems. The one difference with the critical incidents log is that it often includes much greater detail than the performance log. As with the performance log, if we use the critical incidents log we should maintain it for all employees, not just those who are performance challenged. Also as with the performance log, the critical incidents log is readily shared with the employee so that there is full transparency regarding what the supervisor is documenting about the employee's performance. Some of the information that we might document within a critical incidents entry includes:

- Date, time, location
- Description of the event
- Names of others, if any, who observed the behavior
- The consequences or outcomes from the employee's actions or behaviors
- What was said to the employee at the time
- Previous discussions, if any, about the incident
- Desirable behavior or outcomes that were encouraged
- Specific performance improvement expectations communicated
- Consequences that were discussed with the employee if performance improvement doesn't occur and follow-up dates set to review progress
- The employee's reaction to the incident, the coaching conversation, or intervention along with expectations resulting from the conversation

E-mail Documentation

This approach involves the supervisor sending an e-mail to the employee documenting significant examples of the employee's behaviors, accomplishments, failures, successes, and so forth. As with the other forms of performance documentation, you would send an e-mail to the employee to document positive performance as well as performance problems or improvement areas. We also might choose to periodically send e-mails to ourselves documenting key conversations, results, agreements and commitments made, and so forth as critical "notes to self." If we use this methodology, we might want to create e-mail folders within our e-mail manager to preserve and organize these documentary notes.

As with the performance and critical incident logs, everything that we e-mail ourselves as a record of the employee's performance should be something that we've also discussed or shared with the employee at the time. Remember, a fearless review means full transparency and no surprises.

Performance Portfolio

The performance portfolio is a folder that both the supervisor and the employee maintain that contains tangible evidence of specific performance accomplishments and outcomes. The portfolio may contain copies of reports, awards, customer feedback, and commendations. Photographs of key events that celebrate or recognize employee contributions and copies of letters or e-mails from key stakeholders or customers can also be included in the portfolio. The portfolio is maintained to provide documentary evidence of goals achieved, milestones reached, commendations received, and so forth. To ensure that the portfolio is reflective of the full array of possible work products, commendations, feedback, and so forth, it's crucial that the employee be actively encouraged to contribute to it.

The purpose of these performance-documenting methods is to help us remember critical events in the employee's work life that enable us to, when needed, give an objective, fair, and full assessment of the employee's overall job performance. Rather than relying upon our memory or letting recent events influence our thinking, the critical incidents diary helps ensure a more fair historical assessment of the employee's work.

We'll use some or all of these methods for documenting performance throughout the performance period, and then, when preparing for the review, we'll go to these sources to help us gain an objective and holistic view of the employee's performance.

Identifying Performance Strengths and Improvement Areas

The next step of the preparation process is pretty straight forward: based upon the array of expectations that we defined at the beginning of the performance period (including any adjustments or additions to the original expectations) and a review of both system-generated and our own documentations of the employee's performance data, we highlight those areas where the employee meets, fails to meet, and exceeds expectations.

Meets Expectations

This condition occurs when the employee's actual performance outcomes match those established at the beginning of the period. Whether these are behavioral or outcome expectations, when the employee does the right things or achieves the desired outcomes overall or in specific performance areas, this is a good thing. Meeting expectations, especially during times of uncertainty and change, workload stress, shifting business priorities, and so forth means that, despite all of the "noise," the employee has stepped up and done what was expected. While we might have hoped that the employee would go above and beyond expectations, meeting expectations needs to be seen as a positive outcome. And, depending upon the challenges the employee may have faced along the way or if he had a history of failing to meet expectations overall or in a specific area in the past, meeting expectations this time around may be worth celebrating as a great success.

Exceeds Expectations

We love it when employees exceed expectations! When they "wow" us with their extraordinary effort and results, we couldn't be more pleased. At the beginning of each performance period we mutually developed and discussed great performance outcomes and goals. As the employee produces great results throughout the performance period and now, at the end of the cycle, it's gratifying to see the employee move beyond expectations. It's crucial that we never take performance above and beyond expectations for granted and that we make an effort during the review to call out and celebrate extraordinary efforts and results.

It's hugely discouraging to employees when we fail to recognize these efforts. A number of years ago the authors were working with a company to revamp its performance management system. As part of that process they interviewed people throughout the organization about their perceptions of the review process and their suggestions for improving it. David, one of the employees interviewed, expressed frustration and anger with the company's review process and his supervisor. Despite going above and beyond expectations to create what he felt were extraordinary outcomes for customers and the company, during his performance review his supervisor rated his overall performance as average—essentially a "meets expectations" rating. David confronted the supervisor about the average rating and offered numerous examples of performance results that were clearly above and beyond the expectations that the two of them had agreed to at the beginning of the year. Susan, David's supervisor, acknowledged that David had indeed exceeded expectations and then added, "But because all of the employees in our unit exceed expectations, it's just what I expect—which is why I rated you 'average.' You are an average performer when I compare you to others on our team." David wasn't satisfied with that explanation and soon left the company. If we want people to do extraordinary work, then we need to recognize and celebrate it.

There is one instance, however, where we might need to temper our applause: when the extraordinary results in one area of the employee's performance come at the expense of another area. For instance, let's return to our example of Brenda from Parts 1 and 2 of this book. Brenda, an accomplished engineer, produced technical drawings at a level that far exceeded expectations and far exceeded what other engineers around her routinely turned in. The problem with all of her extraordinary work in this area, unfortunately, was that she routinely missed deadlines, and the hours spent in drafting drove the costs up for her clients. So while Tom, her supervisor, valued the quality of her work, he also felt that she actually needed to scale back her drafting hours and quality to "meets expectations" rather than continue to invest time and effort into creating drawings that were far more detailed and precise than needed or wanted. While it would be tough for Tom to ask Brenda to scale back her quality, he really needed her to do so to ensure that she met other expectations that were equally important to the company and client: on-time delivery and reasonable costs.

When employees exceed expectations in a way that is worth celebrating, it's also critical that we examine the factors that led to their success overall or in specific areas. It might be helpful to review the common success factors that were highlighted in Chapter 12.

Fails to Meet Expectations

This is the area that's the least satisfying for all concerned. When an employee's performance behaviors or outcomes somehow miss the expectation targets established at the beginning of a performance period, the resulting gap becomes an area of particular scrutiny. When employees don't meet expectations, it means that something isn't being done in terms of quality and quantity or done at the right time such that there is likely to be a negative consequence for the employee's team members, customers, and, very likely, the company as a whole. If the employee isn't fulfilling the core purpose and function of an entire job or some aspect of the job, there is a problem.

There are, of course, gradations of failing to meet expectations. The failure can simply be a small matter of slightly missing the target with only a modest adjustment required to bring performance back to where it needs to be, or it can be a consequential failure that creates significant problems for a team, for customers, or for the company. So not all fails-to-meet assessments are the same, which means our response as a supervisor needs to reflect the nature and degree of the performance gap.

Regardless of the size of the gap, however, when our assessment of the employee is fails to meet expectations overall or in a specific area, our next step needs to be exploring the causes of the less-than-desirable performance behaviors or results. For, as we learned in Chapter 12, in order for an employee to improve performance overall or in a specific dimension, the underlying causes of the problem need to be identified. To begin with, it might be helpful to review the range of causes of performance challenges that we highlighted in Chapter 12. To help the employee improve her performance, we might need to work with her to first identify the causes of the problem and then construct an action plan for addressing these causes.

Along with exploring causation of the employee's performance challenges, it's also important that we identify any mitigating circumstances that, despite both our and the employee's best efforts, may be negatively affecting the employee's performance. These circumstances might include such system issues as shifting organizational resources or priorities, difficult clients, team dysfunction, a counterproductive organizational culture, and poor quality information or materials. By surfacing mitigating circumstances—many of which may be outside of the employee's sphere of influence—we'll have a better understanding of the context of an employee's performance and be better able to build an improvement plan that moves the employee in the right direction to achieve better results.

At this step of preparing for the review we've gained important insights into how the employee is performing compared to expectations, and we've also developed a preliminary understanding of the factors that may be either contributing to the employee's success or causing him to miss critical performance targets. Our next step is to identify and develop specific goals to explore during the coaching conversation.

14

IDENTIFYING AND DEVELOPING GOALS FOR THE COACHING CONVERSATION

> *It's not enough to be industrious; so are the ants. What are you industrious about?*
>
> —Henry David Thoreau

At the core of performance coaching and the performance coaching conversation is the goal of maintaining an employee's great performance or moving performance to a new level. To achieve these overarching aims, the supervisor approaches each coaching opportunity and coaching conversation with an employee by asking a few key questions: As a result of this performance coaching conversation, what do I hope the employee will keep doing or do differently in the future? What is my goal for this conversation? And what goals do I want to help the employee develop as a result?

These forward-looking questions relate to the forward-looking performance coaching conversation process that we discussed in Chapter 10, which focuses on establishing and developing a set of goals that support the employee's future development and contributions to customers, coworkers, and the company as a whole. There are two broad types of forward-looking goals that we should consider as we try to maintain or improve an employee's performance in the future: *outcome* goals and *process* goals.

Performance Outcome Goals

The outcome goals relate to specific performance deliverables or outcomes where, at the end of the next performance period, something of value is created through the employee's work. As supervisors it's important that we take the time to go into the performance coaching conversation with a thoughtful set of outcome goals. We are suggesting a *set* of goals because the performance coaching conversation offers us a chance to gain a comprehensive view of our employee's work performance and then, based upon this view, develop a suite of goals that offers a comprehensive strategy for increasing the employee's performance contributions.

We believe that most performance coaching conversations should include all or at least most of these four kinds of outcome goals.

Maintain Performance Strengths

For this goal we are interested in working with the employee to create a plan to help him continue performing at his current level in a given area or overall. We also want to see the employee remain committed and motivated to sustaining this level of job performance. Maintaining or sustaining performance might also be a critical goal to consider if the employee is likely to face resource reductions or increases in workload. Finally, maintaining existing performance strengths may be critical if we are also asking the employee to improve in another area. What we don't want is for an employee to shift all of his energy to an improvement area and then lose ground where he was previously strong.

Specific questions to explore as we examine employee performance strengths might include: What is the employee doing right? What is going well with the employee's performance? What should the employee keep doing? What is the significant positive value that this employee's performance brings to the organization?

Improve Performance

Whenever the employee comes up short on meeting performance expectations, this is the outcome goal that's most appropriate. The goals that we and the employee create in this area seek to close the employee's overall performance gap or enhance performance in specific areas where it is falling short of expectations. A related improvement goal would be for the employee to increase her commitment to meeting or exceeding performance expectations. The eventual action plans that result from these improvement goals would need to identify the desired performance target, identify and address obstacles to goal attainment, and outline the steps both the employee and supervisor will take to enable the employee to achieve the goal.

Specific questions to explore as we examine employee performance improvement might include: What isn't going well or being done right? What isn't working? What data suggest that the employee's performance isn't what it should be? Why is improvement in this area necessary? What are the likely causes of the employee's declining performance or missing a performance target? What must be done to correct the problem? What can I, as the supervisor, do to assist the employee with improving in this area? What are my expectations for the future? How quickly will the employee's performance need to improve in this area? What are the consequences for the organization and for the employee if he continues to have difficulties in this area?

Accept New Responsibilities

Rarely do things stay the same in organizations today. New strategic priorities and business challenges periodically cascade down throughout the organization causing divisions, departments, teams, and individuals to shift directions and often take on new responsibilities. The performance coaching conversation presents the perfect time to explore these new directions with each of our employees. This outcome goal is future oriented in that it doesn't involve evaluating the employee's past performance; instead, it suggests a new direction for the employee's work going forward. The new responsibilities or duties that we'd like our employee to accept reflect new and emerging issues, priorities, or goals for our department, the organization as a whole, or for her specific job. In addition, as with the two previous outcome goals, we'll want the employee to accept these new duties, responsibilities, and directions with a high degree of ownership, commitment, and motivation.

Specific questions to explore as we examine potential new directions in the employee's performance might include: What changes are occurring within and outside of the organization that will likely have an impact on how this employee's work is performed or on his performance outcomes? What specific changes should the employee prepare for and respond to? How are the new responsibilities that are being added different from past expectations? To what extent do the new responsibilities change the job scope and authority—and therefore have an impact on compensation and other human resource issues? What will the employee have to learn to be successful in this new performance area, and how might I and the organization support the employee acquiring the new skills and knowledge? What new behaviors and actions will the employee have to learn and demonstrate to fulfill these new responsibilities? How can I and others help the employee succeed in this new area? How much transition time should I grant the employee while she learns the new responsibilities before I hold her accountable for results?

Grow or Move the Job to a New Level

The last of the four outcome goals involves challenging employees who are performing well to push their performance to a higher level. We might believe that an employee is capable of much more than what he has already achieved; this goal pushes him to ramp up performance to a level that's more reflective of what we think he is able to accomplish. Our primary objective is not simply to push the employee harder but to achieve even better outcomes for customers, coworkers, and the organization. By challenging our employees to achieve even more, we enhance their value to the organization, and our entire organization continues to improve and grow. This is what we might call the continuous improvement goal; we don't settle for maintaining our strengths but instead build upon these strengths to continue growing our quality, productivity, efficiency, customer service, and so forth. And, again, part of this "new-level" goal involves getting the employee to take the initiative to grow his job and enhance his performance outcomes.

Specific questions to explore as we investigate ways to develop the employee's continuous performance improvement goals might include: Does the employee take the lead in suggesting ways to enhance his performance? How could this employee enhance his overall performance on one or more specific performance dimensions? How can I, as a supervisor, enable the employee to move his performance to the next level? Are we fully tapping the skills and knowledge of this employee to provide the greatest value to our customers, clients, teams, and entire organization?

So, as we pull our thoughts together prior to the fast-approaching performance coaching conversation, one of our key tasks is to identify our suite of tentative outcome goals that are appropriate to our assessment of the employee's strengths and improvement areas and the emerging issues and challenges that both the employee and the organization may face in the next performance period. We might, for example, identify that the employee is doing a fine job in four core areas and, as a result, we might tentatively consider four maintain-performance goals for the employee's next performance period. At the same time, our analysis of the employee's performance might lead us to identify one area where the employee needs to improve performance to more consistently meet performance expectations. So we would tentatively identify one improve-performance goal to discuss with the employee during the performance coaching conversation. Finally, we might also tentatively identify one new-responsibility goal to explore with the employee based upon some new strategic directions that our company will be taking over the next year and one growth

171

or improvement goal that challenges the employee to move his good performance to an even higher level for a specific dimension.

All of the goals that we've identified at this point are *tentative* in that until we actually conduct the performance coaching conversation with the employee, we can't know for sure if these are the right outcome goals. If we approach the coaching conversation using the collaborative mindset, we will go into the coaching conversation with our own ideas while still remaining open and receptive to what the employee has to say. For despite the no-surprises approach we've taken throughout this book, who is to say that the two of you might not end up developing an entirely different set of outcome goals based upon the give and take during the coaching conversation?

Remember Brenda and her supervisor Tom from our earlier chapters? If Tom had spent some time in advance of his coaching conversation with Brenda really thinking through and developing a tentative set of outcome goals for the conversation and for Brenda's future performance, he might have come up with the following:

- Two maintain-performance goals: Brenda would continue her high-quality technical drawings and her sharing of skills with her coworkers.

- Two improve-performance goals: She would work to increase her on-time deliverables (in part by actually reducing the level of detail in her technical drawings) and strengthen her relationships with customers.

- One new-responsibility goal: She would formally take on a lead-worker responsibility for newly hired engineers—especially in relation to passing on her attention to detail and accuracy (bounded by her new sensitivity to on-time deliverables and customer responsiveness).

- One growth goal: She would develop greater expertise in 3D modeling.

Tom's outcome goals would remain tentative until he and Brenda actually have their coaching conversation. But having done a thoughtful analysis of Brenda's performance and identified an array of possible outcome goals, Tom is in a good position to engage Brenda constructively on how she can continue to bring value to her work—as long as he maintains a collaborative mindset and is truly open to hearing Brenda's perspective.

Performance Process Goals

The performance coaching conversation also presents an opportunity to discuss and reinforce a variety of performance process goals. Process goals deal with relationships: the relationship between the employee and her job, her supervisor, and the organization. While process goals are not the primary focus of the performance coaching conversation, they are an integral part of the conversation because all of these relationships are critically important if an employee is expected to achieve great performance.

Build Greater Ownership for Performance

As we discussed in Chapter 12, the most successful performers become successful in part because they take full responsibility for their own performance. They don't look elsewhere for their success. And when people have greater ownership, they tend to be better at problem solving, exploring root causes of performance challenges, taking responsibility for fixing things that aren't right, and taking the initiative to do what needs to be done to achieve the goal. For this reason, one of our goals as a supervisor should almost always include strengthening employee ownership of the job and performance.

If this is one of the process goals that we decide to discuss during the coaching conversation, then a portion of the conversation should be dedicated to discussing what job ownership looks like to the employee, what might be holding the employee back from greater ownership, the degree to which the employee feels fully responsible for performance results, and so forth. To build greater employee ownership for performance this needs to be part of our coaching conversation.

Build Greater Commitment to the Job and the Organization

When we work with supervisors to help them improve the quality of their coaching conversations, we always steer them away from focusing on an employee's commitment level to the job or the organization. We make the case that it's performance that matters most, not the employee's commitment levels. When supervisors focus too much energy on the employee's commitment level, the coaching conversation often goes like this:

"The problem, as I see it John," the supervisor says, "is that you aren't bringing your full commitment to your job every day."

"I am too!" says John.

"But I don't really see it," says the supervisor.

"I'm just as committed to this work as you are," snaps John.

And on and on it goes. Both the supervisor and John argue about John's commitment level rather than focusing their collective energy on what matters most: John's actual performance results.

The irony is that while we urge supervisors *not* to focus on commitment and instead zero in on performance results, commitment is actually pretty important. It's hard for an employee to become a star performer or achieve great performance if she isn't committed to a job or the organization. If an employee's heart isn't in the work, the results will likely show it. So while we do care about commitment, we don't want it to be the primary focus during the coaching conversation. How might we structure the conversation in such a way that we explore the employee's commitment levels without distracting from the primary focus of performance results? We recommend that supervisors explore employee commitment toward the end of the conversation and do it in a way that is truly conversational such as: "Talk to me about your level of commitment to the job and to this organization. What strengthens your commitment level here, and what weakens it? What could you do and what could I do to enhance your commitment to your job and this organization?"

Strengthen Our Performance Partnership

In our experience working with hundreds of supervisors and employees, the relationship that is often the most important to an employee's performance results is the employee's relationship with his supervisor. As we discussed in Chapter 11, the partnership for performance between the supervisor and the employee is the foundation upon which an employee can achieve great performance. A strong partnership enables great performance through the free flow of information, a willingness to trust and challenge each other, an openness to new ideas, an ability to learn from mistakes rather than fear them, and so forth. Without this strong partnership there is little communication, lower levels of trust, a lack of understanding, and anxiety and even fear due to the uncertainty. This is why a strong partnership between the supervisor and the employee matters.

If we want our employees to achieve great performance, then we need to identify strengthening our partnerships with them as one of our goals. This might include wanting to see our coaching partnership become stronger and more effective; wanting to see both of us making active investments in building our working relationship; and wanting more honest communication, greater levels of trust and respect, and a growing confidence in our performance partnership.

As with the discussion of commitment and ownership, the discussion of strengthening the performance partnership should occur toward the end of the performance coaching conversation. Once the primary discussion of the employee's performance and the resulting set of outcome goals are complete, we can then turn our attention to ways to strengthen the performance partnership. Some of the questions you might explore with the employee include: What do you see as the strength of our partnership? Where do you think our partnership could be strengthened? Am I available when you need guidance and direction? Do you generally feel comfortable approaching me with questions and issues? If there was one thing that each of us could do to strengthen our working relationship, what would it be?

Identify System Barriers and Challenges

Our final process goal to explore during the coaching conversation provides both the employee and the supervisor with the opportunity to identify and discuss system barriers, obstacles, and challenges that may have negatively affected the employee's performance historically as well as those that may negatively affect the employee's performance in the next performance period.

Our goal for exploring system barriers might include wanting to better understand barriers to the employee's performance that may be due to our own actions or inactions; identifying other factors within the larger performance management system or the organization that may be negatively affecting the employee's performance; investigating what we may need to do differently to support the employee's performance improvement, growth, and development; and being better able to separate out the employee's individual effort from potential system causes of things gone wrong.

Some system barrier questions to explore with the employee might include: Have you run into any barriers to your performance outside of our department? Are you getting the information that you need to do your job well? Are others on the team and in the organization helping you to get the results that we're hoping for? Do you have all of the resources and tools you need to achieve your performance goals?

As with the outcome goals, it's desirable that we enter the performance coaching conversation ready to explore multiple process goals. We believe that, in most situations, all four types of goals really should be part of the conversation: a goal to strengthen job ownership, a goal to build commitment to the job and the organization, a goal to enhance the partnership between the employee and the supervisor, and a goal to surface system barriers to the employee's performance. While during the coaching conversation these process goals should take second place to the primary focus on performance outcomes, we think that they are, nonetheless, crucial to turning good or even mediocre performers into star-level employees. The collaborative mindset depends upon and facilitates a rich exchange of information between the employee and the supervisor. The process goals discussed in this section contribute to this flow of information, leading to greater understanding and compassion for both parties in the partnership for performance.

Making Our Goals SMART

As you finalize your suite of tentative outcome and process goals in preparation for the performance coaching conversation, you will need to take special care to ensure that the goals that you have developed have enough depth and meaning to resonate with your employees. The best way to do this is to make the goals SMART. The SMART acronym has been around for years as a framework for creating goals that are more likely to be understood and actionable by others and measurable by all parties. There are multiple versions of this acronym; here is what we see as the most useful one to help guide ourselves and our employees in the goal-setting process:

S

The S stands for specific. A specific goal zeros in on something that is well defined rather than broad and amorphous. So instead of "improve your customer service skills" the goal would say, "improve your response time and answer accuracy when replying to customer questions." The S can also stand for significant and stretching—significant in that the goal is important and matters and stretching in that the goal challenges the person taking it on to push herself somewhat beyond her comfort level. A specific, significant, and stretching goal has clarity and focus (the person enacting the goal knows exactly what's expected), achieving the goal matters, and the goal challenges the person to stretch in a new way.

M

The *M* stands for measurable. This aspect of SMART matters a lot because if we can't measure goal attainment, then we won't know when we've been successful. So instead of "the customer will be satisfied" the goal would say, "the level of customer satisfaction will rise from a 4.5 to a 5.0 on a 6-point scale." The *M* can also stand for meaningful, which, along with significant from the *S*, suggests that success with the goal moves performance forward in a meaningful way.

Years ago we worked with a manager who was struggling to turn a marginal employee into a more productive one. This employee routinely missed deadlines, had poor relationships with his team members, always blamed others for his performance problems, and also kept a very cluttered and disorganized work area. To start somewhere, the manager zeroed in on the employee's messy desk and gave the person a goal: clean your desk by the end of the week! While the employee was able to comply with the specific and measurable goal, achieving the goal made absolutely no difference whatsoever on what really mattered: deadlines, working relationships, and taking responsibility for performance problems. While measurable, it wasn't meaningful.

It is challenging to establish goals that are both measurable and meaningful—not everything that is measurable is meaningful, and not everything that is meaningful is easily measurable. But by paying attention to both meanings of the *M* our goal setting is destined to improve.

A

The *A* stands for accepted. When employees actively choose to accept goals, they are much more likely to view them as their own. Here is where the enacting behavior "share decision making and action planning" of the collaborative mindset plays a central role. If we truly want the employee to own a performance goal, then the goal needs to be mutually developed rather than imposed by the supervisor. And, as we discussed earlier in this book, when there is greater employee ownership, a whole host of positive outcomes follow that make great performance a more likely result.

The A can also stand for appropriate. Within the SMART context, appropriate means that the goal is suitable for both the employee and the situation. The employee has the right skills and knowledge to take on the goal, and it's the right goal for the employee to pursue because it's appropriate for the work that she does and the expectations set before her. It contributes to the larger goal of moving the employee toward great performance and becoming a star performer.

R

The R stands for realistic. Being realistic matters because if the goal is too much of a stretch for the employee or not anchored to a support system that enables the employee to achieve the goal, there's a good chance that the employee may fail at accomplishing the desired results. It's critical to work collaboratively with the employee when setting a goal to ensure that the employee's competence and confidence are present. If they are not, either modify the goal or bolster the employee's skills or self-confidence (or both).

The R can also stand for results oriented. Within our SMART context this means that at the end of the process the goal generated a positive change—results that matter. Goals that generate action alone without meaningful results are a distraction at best and at worst undermine more important goals by diverting the performer's energy.

T

The T stands for time based or time bound. Just achieving a goal is often only part of what the customer, team, or organization needs. If the employee hits the performance target but accomplishes the task three weeks late such that customers were not well served, team members were not able to do their jobs well, or an organizational opportunity was lost, then the overall result was a failure. Establishing time expectations and parameters is a crucial component of most effective goals. A time-based goal statement might say, "Complete the customer assessment process and develop recommendations for action no later than July 15th." With this degree of time specificity, the performer knows exactly when the task needs to be completed.

The *T* can also stand for a related concept: timely. When a goal is timely, it is exactly what the employee needs to be working on right now to best help the team or the organization solve a problem, seize an opportunity, or achieve a larger goal. Similar to time based, timely means that if the goal isn't accomplished at the right time, the employee's effort and results may be less useful to the team or organization.

The Next Step

We're just about ready to have our performance coaching conversation with the employee. We've reviewed the performance expectations set at the beginning of the performance period, we've explored the factors behind the employee's successes and identified possible causes that might explain the gaps between expectations and results, and we've developed a suite of SMART outcome and process goals that will be a major focus for our coaching conversation. There are two more critical steps we need to take before having that face-to-face conversation: completing a draft version of the organization's official appraisal form and getting the backing and support of our manager. Let's turn to Chapter 15 to discuss completing a draft edition of the official appraisal form as a critical next step before actually conducting the coaching conversation.

ACTIONS TO TAKE TO START MOVING IN THE RIGHT DIRECTION

> *Life is ten percent what happens to you and ninety percent how you respond to it.*
>
> —Lou Holtz, American Football Coach

How to Approach the Appraisal Form

Most organizations have their own performance management system, which also includes the official appraisal form that needs to be completed by the supervisor, reviewed with the employee, and submitted to human resources. Some organizations don't have any organization-wide system, structure, or process in place, leaving it to each division or department to create the system and appraisal form that's the best fit for the organizational unit. If your organization is silent on the process and has no official appraisal form, then you may be on your own to figure out how to document the results of your performance coaching conversation.

Whatever your situation, we believe that the form you use doesn't matter as much as the quality of the conversation. However, the appraisal form does matter if it actually gets in the way of the conversation. When the form itself causes people to shift into the my-way mindset and veer toward defensiveness or go on the offensive, we need to take proactive steps to reduce the undermining "form effect" during the performance coaching conversation.

Appraisal forms that render a final judgment on the employee's work are particularly problematic distractions from the coaching conversation. If we rate an employee as "fails to meet expectations," "needs improvement," or even "meets expectations" and the employee sees herself as having worked hard and believes that she went above and beyond yet had to deal with significant challenges that hurt her performance, she is likely to be frustrated and lose motivation. Imagine trying to have a meaningful conversation about the past year with an employee in that frame of mind. How successful is the conversation likely to be at engaging the employee and encouraging her to work collaboratively with the supervisor to set goals for the next year?

To reduce the form effect as much as possible, we recommend trying to separate the form from the performance coaching conversation. When we separate the form from the conversation, it allows both the supervisor and the employee to keep their focus on the conversation instead of on what boxes are checked and what the final evaluation or judgment is. If we don't separate the form from the conversation, the form is likely to become the focus rather than the sharing, understanding, gaining insight, and learning that are the foundation of an effective, forward-looking process and conversation.

It's for this reason we recommend that if your official appraisal form has a final-judgment section where you are asked to give a single final rating of the employee's overall performance, you might approach the process in the following way:

1. Complete the form with the word DRAFT stamped or marked on every page. This is a reminder to yourself and

lets the employee know that you are open to the possibility of changing any of our assessment findings based upon what you learn in the conversation.

2. If possible, leave blank or unchecked any final overall assessment section. This says to the employee and to you that this final assessment rating will be dependent upon what we learn during the conversation. Depending upon how your organization's appraisal form is structured, you may also want to leave unchecked the ratings on individual performance dimensions and instead focus your conversation on narrative descriptions and bullet point observations for each performance dimension.

3. Consider using the job description or your preparatory notes as the foundation for the conversation rather than the appraisal form in order to keep the focus on the conversation. The strength of using the form is that it can often bring structure to the process, but if it has the chance of getting in the way, try creating your own structure—perhaps along the lines we have proposed in the outcome and process goals section of this chapter. You may also want to consider focusing the first part of the coaching conversation on your preparatory notes and the last section on the official form. Whatever route you follow, strive to prevent the form from becoming a barrier to communication, understanding, insight, and learning.

4. Schedule a brief follow-along meeting with the employee at least two days after the performance coaching conversation. At this follow-along meeting you will share your final assessment rating with the employee—after having had a chance to reflect upon what you learned during the coaching conversation. This separation of the discussion of your final rating from the coaching conversation encourages both the employee and you to focus on what each is learning from the other rather than on the rating.

As we learned in Chapter 10, the focus of the performance coaching conversation is on the future. When the appraisal form requires a backward-looking summary judgment ("I've rated your overall performance a 3 on a 6-point scale."), be extra careful about how we manage the process. Yes, we may end up giving the employee the same overall summary rating after the coaching conversation as you were inclined to before the conversation, but if you've been genuinely open to hearing something new that could change the assessment, then the employee is more likely to believe that the process was fair and that he had an opportunity to actually influence our rating.

So, whether or not you use the appraisal form at some point during the coaching conversation or instead move the coaching conversation along using the job description or our preparatory notes, the focus of the conversation is on insight and learning, not on the form, the checkboxes, or the past.

Increasing the Frequency of Your Performance Coaching Conversations

As we've noted throughout this book, performance management and performance coaching are not singular events during a year. Effective performance management is something that every supervisor should invest in every day, and coaching involves the supervisor making investments in a strong relationship with each employee throughout the year.

For these reasons, we think that it's crucial that you conduct relatively frequent, brief, and informal performance coaching conversations with each employee. By scheduling check-in coaching conversations on a regular basis—perhaps every four to six weeks or so (and more often if needed)—you keep the lines of communication with the employee open. This provides an opportunity for each of you to comfortably raise issues, questions, and challenges related to the employee's performance goals and outcomes before they become bigger issues. It also gives you both the chance to work collaboratively to solve challenging performance issues and then to make adjustments as necessary to the employee's goals or the level of support that you or the organization provide for the employee. By having these frequent check-in coaching conversations there is likely to be much less fear because performance issues, challenges, and problems are identified and addressed earlier than if the conversation were to happen only once or twice a year. As a result, there will likely be fewer surprises and disappointments for either party because both the supervisor and the employee are touching base and talking about meaningful performance issues on a regular basis.

We believe that increasing the frequency of these brief and informal check-in performance coaching conversations will contribute significantly to the employee's ability to achieve great performance. What might a check-in coaching conversation look like? It could involve something as simple as the supervisor asking the employee, "How are things going for you? Have you had any setbacks or significant successes since we last talked? What's going well, and what's not going well?" Or it could involve the employee asking the supervisor, "I'd like your help sorting through some of the issues on this project. Do you have any thoughts on how I might approach this?"

Frequent coaching conversation check-ins keep the performance partnership strong by helping ensure that both parties have a shared understanding of the employee's performance expectations and the progress he is making toward realizing these expectations. This allows performance issues to be addressed before they become major problems and enables both the employee and the supervisor to take corrective action if necessary to get performance back on track. Frequent coaching conversations are also likely to make it easier to talk about uncomfortable things—such as performance failures—because there is greater communication, openness, empathy, and trust between the parties. The collaborative mindset thrives on frequent interaction where there is a free-flowing exchange of valid information. The my-way mindset tends to thrive when the interactions are infrequent, which creates ample opportunities for misunderstandings, assumptions, and judgments that in turn can lead to counterproductive, self-fulfilling, and self-sealing thinking by both parties.

The formal performance coaching conversations at the midpoint and end of the employee's performance period take on a slightly different tone: these are a bit more structured, as the supervisor and employee come together to review the employee's performance on each of her essential job functions and the performance goals established at the beginning of the period. As we'll discover in Chapter 16, the more formal *summary* coaching conversation focuses the employee's and supervisor's attention on developing a suite of outcome and process goals for either the balance of the performance period (for a midpoint conversation) or the next performance period (for a final summary conversation). It's also during or following these more formal summary performance coaching conversations that the official review forms might be completed to document the employee's performance outcomes.

We hope that the key take-away from this discussion about the frequency of performance coaching conversations is that doing them more often is likely to reduce fear and increase the strength of the performance partnership. Getting rid of the fear and building a strong partnership are both crucial to keeping employees on track for meeting or even exceeding their performance expectations.

Getting Management Support for Your Actions

We've done our homework and, going into this coaching conversation, we have a solid foundation for a successful dialogue about the employee's performance. And, because of the data-gathering work we've done throughout the year and our assessment of how well the employee is achieving his goals, we have a good sense of the issues that we'll be exploring during the conversation, the goals that we hope to discuss, and an idea of some possible actions that we're prepared to take following the conversation. The issues we might raise could include celebrating and rewarding success, guiding the employee toward improvement, nudging him in a new direction, challenging the employee to ramp performance up to a new level, strengthening the partnership for performance, or putting pressure on an employee to significantly improve performance.

While we may have a tentative plan for the coaching conversation, we're still not quite ready to actually have the conversation. Before we initiate the face-to-face performance discussion with the employee we'll first need to brief our manager to ensure that she is fully supportive of what we want to accomplish and the organizational implications emerging from the conversation. Some of the issues that we might want to first run past our manager before the coaching conversation include:

- Share our goals for the employee's performance and ensure that the manager supports these goals.

- Gather additional data on the employee's performance based upon the manager's observations and perceptions.

- Share our tentative overall performance rating (acknowledging that it may change based upon the dialogue with the employee) and ask for the manager's support for this tentative rating.

- Explore the potential consequences for the employee and the organization (e.g., salary increase, merit awards, and reduction in the employee's autonomy or authority) from any overall performance rating—and get the manager's support for these consequences.

- Identify emerging business priorities and needs that should be reflected in the employee's future work priorities and goals.

- Discuss possible corrective action that may emerge from the coaching conversation and get the manager's full support for these actions.

- Identify and discuss potential discipline that may be on the horizon for the employee if, in the short run, the employee's performance doesn't improve.

- Identify whether human resources should be consulted to help ensure a successful process. Potential issues to explore with human resources might include developing a corrective action plan, ensuring consistency and equity for proposed merit increases or sanctions, and providing reasonable accommodations under the Americans with Disabilities Act along with modifying the position description and exploring the HR implications of doing so.

- Discuss additional support and other resources that we might need to provide to enable great performance from this employee and other employees on our team.

The foundation for a successful coaching conversation is now in place. All of the work that we've done to this point has helped us develop a clear path toward helping the employee strengthen his future performance and perhaps move to star-performer status. We've discussed our tentative plan with our manager, and she has shared her thoughts and suggestions and is fully supportive of what we're trying to do.

It's now time to conduct the face-to-face coaching conversation. As we approach the coaching conversation, utilizing the powerful behaviors of the collaborative mindset, we have our plan and we also are ready to gain new insights and learn from what the employee is ready to share with us.

Let's move into Chapter 16, where we learn how to conduct the fearless review by transforming it into a collaborative conversation where both parties learn and grow.

PUTTING YOUR HARD WORK INTO ACTION

We shall not cease from exploration
And the end of all our exploring
Will be to arrive where we started
And know the place for the first time.
—T. S. Eliot, "Little Gidding," the last of his *Four Quartets*

It's in this chapter that all of what you've learned in this book comes together. There's a good chance that you purchased *Fearless Performance Reviews* just for this chapter—a roadmap for beginning, navigating, and bringing closure to a performance review. But, as we hope you've found out, conducting a fearless coaching conversation involves much more than just having a script to follow or a set of phrases to draw from. While a script and phrasebook can be helpful, it's far more important to have a facilitative mindset and a deep understanding of the larger context within which employee performance takes place. When you bring together the collaborative mindset, the great performance management cycle and its focus on employee ownership and responsibility for performance, the ability to effectively discover the causes behind performance success and failure, and a focus on defining outcome and process goals for the coaching conversation, the result is not just a fearless review but a powerful coaching conversation that is more likely to cultivate star-level performance in every employee.

As we briefly mentioned in Chapter 10, there are two types of performance coaching conversations. While both use an informal and conversational approach, one has more structure than the other. The frequent and more informal check-in performance coaching conversation is less structured and is largely focused on the supervisor and employee staying connected and engaged with each other throughout the performance period. The more formal summary performance coaching conversation consciously examines each of the employee's core job responsibilities and reviews the employee's progress at meeting these responsibilities and achieving the performance goals established at the beginning of the performance period. Summary coaching conversations are typically done at a midpoint and at the end of the performance period but can be done more often if the employee needs more involved coaching and direction or is perhaps struggling with some aspect of performance.

The performance coaching conversation that we introduce in this chapter presents the more structured approach—the summary coaching conversation. While we encourage you to use elements of this more structured approach in your more frequent and less formal check-in coaching conversations, you won't necessarily be exploring all of the issues and questions that we introduce in this chapter. The check-in conversations should be more casual and focused on staying in touch rather than on examining every aspect of the employee's performance.

There are two steps that need to occur before you and the employee sit down for the face-to-face conversation: preparing the employee for the performance coaching conversation and finalizing your own thoughts following a gaining-support meeting with your manager (which we discussed in Chapter 15).

Let's first explore ways to get employees to take full ownership and responsibility for their performance coaching conversations so that they can actually take the lead during the conversation.

Preparing the Employee for the Coaching Conversation

As we discussed in Chapter 11 and throughout this book, achieving great performance is each employee's responsibility. This responsibility includes all of the ingredients necessary for achieving success within the great performance management cycle: defining great performance outcomes; establishing goals that move the employee toward these outcomes; acquiring the support, resources, and tools to get the job done; and taking the lead responsibility for evaluating performance results and then taking action for sustaining performance success or moving closer to success.

If we've done a good job of facilitating employee ownership of great performance throughout the performance period, then the employee has already taken a lead role in most of the steps within the great performance management cycle listed above. As we move into the summary performance coaching conversation the final two aspects of employee ownership within this cycle come to the fore: the employee taking the lead in both evaluating her performance and in developing insight and action plans for sustaining or achieving success in the next performance period.

Getting an employee to take an effective lead role in this process doesn't happen just because we ask him to. We may need to provide the employee with guidance and structure to help him navigate the new approach. Giving employees a template or roadmap with which to lead the summary performance coaching conversation is especially important for those employees who historically have never been asked to actively participate in their performance reviews.

We recommend that supervisors meet briefly with each employee to highlight how the summary performance coaching conversation will work (with the employee taking the lead role) and ask the employee to do her own preparations in advance of the conversation—just as the supervisor will be doing. During this brief preconversation meeting, we think that it's especially useful for supervisors to provide each employee with the following:

- A copy of the employee's job description, which, ideally, already includes the great performance outcome expectations that the employee took part in defining. This document should list the essential job functions in detail along with the percentage of the employee's effort and time that is recommended to be dedicated to each essential job function (the percentages help establish priorities for the employee's work).

- A copy of the results and goals from previous performance coaching conversations. These results and goals should include those from the more formal endpoint or midpoint summary conversation and any additional conversations during the performance period where goals and action plans were developed.

- If desired, a copy of the organization's formal performance review form—ideally with the performance goals for the performance period just completed already listed on the form. Depending upon the process that you decide to follow or the process expectations of your organization, you may want to ask the employee to actually complete the form as part of his self-assessment.

- A copy of the Performance Coaching Conversation Preparations Guide (Figure 16.1). This guide helps employees reflect back upon and examine their performance over the performance period (3, 6, or 12 months) and, based upon that reflection, identify some possible next steps that they and their supervisor can take in the next performance period to sustain or improve their performance.

Reflect back upon the past three months, six months, or year, and explore your work performance and outcomes as you consider the following questions:

What is going well with the job and Why is it going well? What about the job is working? What are some of the good things that are happening in each of your job responsibility areas? What recent accomplishments are you especially proud of? What parts of your job do you feel especially good about? Are there any strength areas where you could further raise the bar on your performance? Why is the job or this aspect of the job going well?

What isn't going well in the job? What aspects of your job aren't working as well as you'd like? What job problems or difficulties in any of your responsibility areas have you experienced lately?

Why isn't this going well? What are the likely causes of performance challenges? If you are experiencing performance challenges, what might be the *causes* of these things not going well?

What changes or improvements could you make in how you approach your job to help you maintain areas where you are strong, move your performance to a new level, or improve things that are not going well? What actions could you take that would enable you to sustain your performance where things are going well? What could you do to build upon your past success and move your performance to a new level? What actions could you take to address the causes of things not going well and which, if you took these actions, would likely improve your future performance outcomes and goals?

How might I (your supervisor) help you to be more successful in your job? What can I do more or less of to enable you to achieve or exceed your performance goals?

What do you see as performance areas where there may be a need for new responsibilities and future growth in your performance? Based upon what you see going on in the organization and in your job, what new directions do you see your position moving in? What new responsibilities should be added to your position in the future? Which responsibilities are *less* important now than previously? How do you see your job changing over the next performance period?

Possible Additional Questions for the More Formal Summary Performance Coaching Conversation:

How would you assess your overall performance and your performance for each of your job and organizational responsibilities? For each responsibility area, to what extent are you exceeding, meeting, or failing to meet your performance goals? What measures are you using to gauge your performance in each area? What factors are supporting or limiting your success in each of these areas?

What are your long-term professional development and career goals? Where do you see yourself five years from now? What's most important to you in your work? What would you most like to accomplish in your work here?

The Performance Coaching Conversation Preparation Guide is intended to encourage critical reflection in the employee and to help him or her prepare for taking a lead role during the coaching conversation. Giving your employee a copy of this preparations guide it is likely to increase his or her comfort level in preparing for the coaching conversation as well as build their confidence for taking a lead role during the conversation.

FIGURE 16.1 Performance Coaching Conversation Preparation Guide

The Performance Coaching Conversation Preparation Guide (a copy of which is also included in the appendix at the back of the book) is intended to encourage critical reflection in employees and to help them prepare for taking a lead role during the coaching conversation. Giving your employee a copy of this preparation guide is likely to increase her comfort level in preparing for the coaching conversation as well as build her confidence for taking a lead role during the conversation.

We recommend that when you give the employee copies of the job description, past goals, blank review form, and preparations guide that you do so with words along these lines:

> *Your summary performance coaching conversation is scheduled for two weeks from now, and I wanted to talk with you briefly to help you prepare for this conversation. As you know, my approach to the performance review involves more of a coaching conversation than a formal review, and I look forward to both of us taking some time to reflect upon your work during the past performance period and to develop some performance goals for the next period.*
>
> *As we have discussed before, I expect and hope that you will take an active role in this coaching conversation and, to the greatest extent possible, I'd like you to actually lead the conversation. To help you prepare for this active role, I'd like you to review and reflect upon this Performance Coaching Conversation Preparation Guide. I think that you'll find that it provides a useful way to structure your performance self-assessment, helps you explore the causes of your performance successes and setbacks, asks you to identify how I can be most helpful to you going forward, and assists you in thinking about next steps and possible goals for the future.*
>
> *I'll be considering the same set of questions in my own assessment of your work efforts over the next couple of weeks. When we come together for this summary performance coaching*

conversation, I expect that both of us will be prepared to talk about where your performance is today and where it can be going forward.

In addition to reflecting on your performance over the past performance period, I will be reviewing the performance log that you know I maintain for all employees who report to me. I will also be reviewing the performance portfolio that I keep for you and all of my employees. As you may recall, the performance portfolio is a place where I retain examples of your work outcomes and documents related to your performance such as, commendations, letters, and e-mails from others. If you have any work products to contribute to this portfolio that would be helpful to me in assessing your work over the performance period, please pass these on to me.

In addition to the Performance Coaching Conversation Preparation Guide, I am giving you copies of your job description, the previous performance goals that you and I developed at the beginning of the performance period, and a blank copy of the performance review form (with your performance goals filled in). All of these should be helpful to you as you pull your thoughts together in preparation for an active role during this coaching conversation.

If, after today, you have any questions about the forthcoming summary performance coaching conversation and your role in it, just stop by, give me a call, or shoot me an e-mail. I want to make sure that both of us are ready to make this conversation a positive and productive one where we both learn something from each other.

Setting or reinforcing employees' expectations for their role during the summary performance coaching conversation is crucial to an effective process. The collaborative mindset encourages us to make the coaching conversation a collaborative one, and, to ensure that it is, employees need to understand what is expected of them during the process and what they need to do in advance of the conversation. If we take steps to ensure that employees have this understanding, then we are more likely to have a fearless conversation that leads to shared understanding, insight, learning, and a positive plan for action going forward.

Finalizing Your Preparations

You have reaffirmed your process and outcome expectations for the summary performance coaching conversation with the employee and you've met with your manager to ensure that she fully supports your tentative assessment findings and goals. The last step you should take before you hold the performance coaching conversation is to review your tentative assessment and goals one last time to make sure that they represent your best thinking and that they have been informed by:

- A collaborative mindset by which you have objectively and holistically reviewed the employee's performance and developed some tentative ideas to explore with the employee.

- Your manager's viewpoint, perspective, and priorities. As we discussed in Chapter 15, your manager may have useful data on the employee's performance to share with you or may have suggestions for new directions or work priorities for the employee in the future.

- If appropriate, suggestions from human resources on how to provide a reasonable accommodation for a disability. Refer the employee to the employee assistance program (EAP) if appropriate, or introduce a corrective action plan as part of the next-steps goals for the employee.

- Any performance data or outcome documentation that the employee may have shared with you recently that you didn't previously have available to you.

In addition, if you have completed a draft version of the formal review form, you'll need to decide if and when you will introduce this during the performance coaching conversation. It's critical that you do so in a collaborative and transparent way. You might decide that, somewhere near the beginning of the coaching conversation, you will tell the employee that you've completed a draft version of the form and that it's in draft form because you expect that it will change based upon what you learn during the conversation. You might add that you're happy to share this draft at the end of the coaching conversation because your preference is to not focus on the form but instead focus on the conversation itself. You can suggest that at the end of the conversation you'd like to schedule a brief follow-along meeting with the employee to review the final version of the form—based upon what you learned during the coaching conversation. You are not unilateral about when and how the form is integrated into the process, however, and if the employee wants to include your draft review form as part of the conversation then you are open to exploring his reasoning for this, explaining your own reasoning, and then coming to a mutual understanding of how best to integrate the form into the process in a way that honors each of your viewpoints.

One final preparation you need to make is ensuring that you've set aside sufficient time for a true dialogue with the employee and that the conversation is conducted in a location where both of you feel comfortable. This means being prepared to silence your phone, turn off e-mail alerts, and block out your schedule so that neither of you will be interrupted by phone calls, e-mail notifications, passers-by, or another appointment that's been scheduled too close to the coaching conversation. It also means working with the employee to choose the meeting space where he as well as you feel most at ease. Your office may be a perfect match for these conditions or a conference room might be better. The two of you can decide what time and location are most conducive for an effective conversation.

Once you've addressed all of these final preparation issues, you're ready for the conversation. With the preparatory work that both you and the employee have done, the actual conversation will be pretty easy. All it takes is beginning on the right foot.

Starting Things Off

The time has come. The employee arrives. You're both ready to jump right in and talk about the past performance period as a bridge to the next performance period. You begin by setting the tone for the rest of the session. Reiterate the reason for the performance coaching conversation, your larger objectives for the session (e.g., a better understanding of his performance, a chance to identify obstacles and barriers to great performance, set new goals for the next performance period, and strengthen your working relationship), your interest in having him take a lead role in the process, and your reasoning behind your desire to have the employee take this lead role.

Here is some sample language that we encourage you to consider as a way to get things moving forward. We aren't offering this as a precise script for you to follow because you need to make this entire process your own. What we are offering is more of a framework for introducing the process and inviting dialogue; we don't expect you to simply adopt our words. With that qualifier, you might consider kicking things off by saying something like this:

As we discussed a couple of weeks ago when we set the date for this summary performance coaching conversation, I'm hoping that today's discussion about your performance over the past performance period will help us both better understand each other's performance aspirations, concerns, needs, and issues. Some of my goals for this session include [list your broad goals here]. In addition, what I find useful about this coaching conversation is that it gives me a chance to clarify my own thoughts, expectations, and perceptions of your performance, and I hope that it does the same for you.

You can depend on me to speak honestly about how I perceive your performance and how I arrived at these thoughts and perceptions. And, in the interest of a collaborative process, I encourage you to do the same. This is especially important if we talk about an issue or area where we disagree. I hope that if we do disagree about something, we each make an effort to understand each other's perspectives and how we each arrived at these perspectives. Because I think our mutual goal is to find a way to maintain and build upon your success here rather than to determine whose point of view is the right one, I hope that you'll join with me in an honest dialogue about your past performance and what's next for your performance going forward.

Does that sound like a fair way to approach this conversation?

As you'll recall, when we first set the date for this coaching conversation, I asked you to think about a number of questions in advance. My intention in asking you to think about these questions was to encourage you to do a self-assessment of your own performance, to encourage critical reflection on your past work, to get you thinking about things that both you and I could do to support your performance in the future, and to encourage you to take a lead role during this conversation—rather than just responding to my assessment of your performance.

Because of my interest in your taking a lead role in this process, my preference is to have you start things off. My reasoning for this reflects my desire to have you take an active role in this process, and also because I'm especially interested in hearing your thoughts about how you see your performance without the influence of my assessment. Once you've had a chance to share your perspective on things, then I'd like to offer my comments and thoughts. Does that sound okay to you? Are you comfortable with this approach?

If the employee's response is that he would rather that you to go first, explore his thinking. Model the collaborative mindset by exploring his reasoning for wanting you to lead the process. Share your own reasoning and intentions again if necessary, and then, after you've discussed each other's reasoning, mutually decide how you will both proceed. Because you want the process to be transparent with no hidden strategy or agenda, you both need to be comfortable with whatever path the two of you decide to take.

While this isn't our preference (for the reasons we've cited above), if the two of you decide that *you* will lead the process with the employee playing a more reactive role, the next question you would have for the employee is:

Because we've decided that I'll lead the process and present my analysis first, with you following with your own assessment, comments, and reactions, where would you like me to begin? Do you want me to start with your performance strengths—where I see you meeting or exceeding expectations? Or would you prefer that I start with my perceptions of your improvement areas?

These questions help you avoid the manipulative sandwich technique that we discussed earlier in the book and invite the employee to take greater ownership of the process—even when you take the lead role.

If, however, (as we hope) you are successful at making the case for having the employee lead the process, and the employee agrees to present his analysis first, you move into the first dialogue about what's going well:

Okay, to start things off, I'd like to hear your thoughts about what is going well in your job—first in general and then about each of your essential job functions.

Exploring Perceptions of Performance Strengths

The employee presents an analysis of what's going well in the job, highlighting performance outcome strengths, accomplishments, great successes, the progress made despite resource constraints, and so forth. This is the employee's opportunity to talk about the successes that he has experienced and to share the factors or causes behind these successes. As the supervisor, you are listening actively with an open mind; you are asking questions, clarifying what he is sharing, asking for greater detail, and inviting a deeper sharing such that you fully hear and understand how the employee perceives his performance strengths and the factors that help explain these successes.

Through active listening, encourage the employee to share performance successes overall and within each of his essential job functions from the job description and to highlight his successes at accomplishing the goals identified at the beginning of the performance period.

Once the employee completes his performance strengths and success factors overview, it's your turn to chime in by affirming the strengths identified by the employee and adding new strength areas that the employee may have missed. Your goal is to achieve a shared understanding of the employee's overall strengths, strengths within each essential job function, and the employee's success in meeting or exceeding the specific performance goals for the performance period as well as a shared understanding of the factors or causes behind all of this success.

Based upon this shared understanding, you and the employee will then mutually identify and discuss performance goals for the forthcoming performance period that maintain or build upon the employee's success by amplifying and reinforcing the success factors. At the end of the performance strengths part of the coaching conversation, the two of you will have identified a set of maintaining or building goals for the employee's future performance.

This is also the time when you can encourage the employee to consider building upon his strengths and moving his performance to a new level—one even closer to great or exceptional performance. Star performers become stars not just by meeting expectations and maintaining their strengths; they keep pushing themselves and their performance by continually raising the bar. It's at this time when you bring in the "grow or move the job to a new level" outcome goals that you identified in your advance planning. Following the approach you used when beginning the discussion of the employee's performance strengths, you again invite the employee to offer some ideas in this area. Here's some sample language you might use:

Thinking about some of your performance strengths that we've discussed, do you see any of these as areas where you are well-positioned to raise the bar on your performance? In other words, are any of these areas where you can raise your performance outcomes to the next level in the forthcoming performance period?

Once you've asked these or similar questions, your focus again shifts to active listening as you draw out the employee's ideas, ask questions, clarify, and paraphrase what you are hearing. You explore the employee's reasoning behind his suggestions and then follow the employee's insights and suggestions with your own—sharing your own reasoning about why the employee ramping up performance in a given area is desirable. And then together you mutually agree upon the raising-the-bar performance outcome goals for the employee's next performance period.

One final point regarding the strengths discussion: as we discussed earlier, you will need to use your judgment as to whether and how you integrate the strengths that you may have previously identified on your draft review form (either a blank one with only the performance goals displayed or a draft version with your tentative assessment). While our recommendation is that you introduce and discuss the review form in a subsequent meeting to enable you to make changes to the form based upon what you learn in the conversation, you and the employee should choose an approach that works best for you. If you decide to introduce your draft review form as part of the strengths discussion, ensure that the employee understands that the form is a draft and that you will likely be making changes to it based upon the coaching conversation.

Exploring Perceptions of Performance Improvement Areas

Once the two of you have completed the strengths discussion, the conversation shifts to focus on areas for improvement. Again you invite the employee to go first by asking him to discuss areas for improvement (what isn't going well) in the job overall and on specific performance dimensions and, for each improvement area, to share his ideas for likely causes of performance problems in these areas.

As the employee begins sharing his perspective, you will again use active listening to gather valid information about what's not going well, explore the employee's thinking behind the causes of the performance challenges that he has identified, and continue verifying your understanding of what you heard. Once the employee has finished identifying his improvement areas and the underlying causes behind these areas, it's time for you to share your list of improvement opportunities. As with strengths, you'll affirm any improvement areas identified by the employee that are also on your list and add new areas that the employee may have missed. You'll also offer your thoughts on the possible causes of the performance challenges that both you and the employee have identified.

As you present your analysis, to ensure that both of you stay in a collaborative frame of mind, it might be most helpful if you:

- Share the data behind your performance observations using specific examples and incidents.

- Identify any assumptions you are making about the employee's performance and ask him for alternative interpretations of these assumptions.

- Provide feedback in a constructive way that focuses on specific, observable, and measurable performance outcomes and behaviors rather than on abstract terms such as commitment, attitude, and dedication.

Through the back-and-forth dialogue, a clear and shared understanding begins to emerge of where the employee could most improve performance and the factors or causes that may be undermining his success in general or on specific performance dimensions. If improvement on specific performance behaviors or outcomes is one of your goals, get the employee to acknowledge that a change in behaviors or performance outcomes is desired and then work with the employee to explore possible actions and strategies for turning the behaviors or outcomes around.

Dealing with Disagreement

If the employee doesn't agree with your perception that there is a problem with performance or that a change in behavior is necessary, use the disagreement as an opportunity to explore each other's reasoning and perceptions at a deeper level. Using your empathy and a desire for understanding, seek to gain greater insight into why the employee doesn't see this area as needing improvement. Explore his view and why it might be different from yours. If, in the end, you remain convinced that the behaviors or performance needs to change, again reiterate the reasons why you think this is so. You might find it helpful to ask the employee to state—in his own words—the consequences of not changing these behavior or outcomes. Explain the reasoning behind your request. Ask the employee to think through these consequences; he might better appreciate the consequences and impact on himself and others after some consideration and introspection. This, we hope, moves the employee in the direction of a free and informed choice—a key value of the collaborative mindset.

If the employee continues to see things differently and doesn't recognize the need for changing his behaviors or outcomes in a specific performance area or overall, explain that you need to see behavioral or outcome changes—that the current performance level isn't acceptable or sustainable. Because, using the collaborative mindset, you are committed to the employee making a free and informed choice, you invite the employee to make a different choice than the one that he is making now. Explain that, from your vantage point, all the choices open to him aren't equal—choosing to perform at the level that you are encouraging him to perform at is likely to lead to a set of positive consequences for him, for the team, for the customers, and for the organization overall. You would add that the employee is free to choose a different path—perhaps sticking with the choices that he has already made—and that choosing this other path has a different set of consequences—consequences that are not likely to be as positive for the employee or others.

We'd encourage you to state that you are open to hearing why the employee insists on choosing a path different from the one you would prefer. By stating that you are willing to listen and be persuaded to change your perceptions and expectations, you demonstrate that you haven't made up your mind. If, however, after exploring the issue further you remain committed to the employee making a choice more aligned with the one you would prefer, we recommend that you explain that if he continues to follow this different path, you may need to make a choice as well—a choice (such as reducing the employee's authority and responsibility, increasing your oversight, or taking the employee off of a high-status project) that may not be aligned with the employee's long-term goals or interests.

When there is a continuing disagreement between both of you, your goal is not necessarily to get the employee to agree with you; your goal is simply to get the employee to behave differently or to achieve different results. He may continue to disagree that a change in behavior or outcomes is necessary and yet, despite this ongoing disagreement, still be expected to do things differently or achieve different results. Obviously, we would like to have our employees take full ownership of and be fully engaged with the performance behaviors and outcomes that are aligned with our needs, but that may not always be possible. The key is that embracing the collaborative mindset doesn't preclude us from increasing pressure on an employee to make different choices. We invite the employee to make different choices, and, if he doesn't, we are free to make our own choices (transparently communicating to the employee the choices we may need to make). Acting in this way doesn't mean that we're moving into unilateral territory—especially when we put all of our cards on the table, explain our reasoning and intentions, and invite the employee to make a free and informed choice as to how he will respond to our preferences. It means that we care about the choices our employee is making and we invite him to choose differently.

Coming to a Mutual Agreement for Performance Improvement

Once you both have a shared understanding of areas for performance improvement and the causes that might be limiting success in these areas, your conversation shifts into problem solving, goal setting, and action planning. While as part of your preparations for the conversation you may have identified some tentative improvement goals, in this segment of the coaching conversation you again invite the employee to take the lead role in exploring goals and action steps. We recommend that you:

- Ask the employee if he understands what the goal is for each performance area and to identify possible actions that he could take to address the underlying causes of the performance issues and move his performance closer to the desired outcome.

- Assist the employee in defining and refining the performance improvement goal by making it a SMART goal (see Chapter 14) and identifying ways that both of you might measure success at achieving the goal.

- Follow the employee's ideas for action with your own. Link your recommendations for action with his ideas as much as possible and explain the reasoning and intentions behind your suggested actions.

The outcome from this phase of your coaching conversation is a set of SMART improvement goals that are mutually developed and agreed upon and focused on moving the employee's performance toward great performance. And if the conversation is informed by the collaborative mindset—at least on your part but ideally the employee's as well—there will be less fear, greater openness to moving forward, and a strong mutual commitment to the employee's future success.

Identifying Areas for Growing the Job or Moving It in a New Direction

In your preparatory work prior to the summary performance coaching conversation you identified goals that sought to maintain or build upon the employee's performance strengths and shore up performance improvement areas. We also encouraged you to consider developing other outcome goals for the coaching conversation that included the employee accepting new responsibilities or pushing the employee's performance in a new direction. Once the two of you have explored the employee's strengths and improvement areas during the coaching conversation and set goals in these areas, it's time to explore this additional outcome goal area.

Just as you did for the discussion of the previous outcome goals, for the accept-new-responsibilities goal, you again invite the employee to lead the way. Your invitation might have you saying something like this:

"One of the questions I asked you to consider prior to today's coaching conversation was whether you saw a need for new responsibilities or growth in your performance for the future. I'm interested in hearing your thoughts on this. What do you see as some possible new directions for your work in the future? What new responsibilities do you see taking on based upon changes that you see occurring within and outside of the organization?"

After you've asked these or similar questions, you again use active listening to draw out the employee's ideas, ask questions, clarify, and paraphrase what you are hearing. For each new direction or responsibility identified by the employee, you'll want to explore his reasoning behind the new direction or shift in responsibilities.

And, again, you then follow the employee's suggestions with your own possible new directions—sharing your reasoning about why the employee's moving performance in a given direction is desirable. Finally, you mutually agree upon the job-growth or new-directions outcome goals for the employee's next performance period.

Discussing Process and Relationship Issues

So far during the coaching conversation you've worked collaboratively with the employee to discuss and develop goals that maintain and build upon the employee's performance strengths, directly tackle performance improvement areas, and grow the job in a new direction. These outcome goals are the primary drivers of your coaching conversation. They are not, however, the only goals you'll want to discuss. As you may recall from Chapter 14, it's also important to include process goals (e.g., employee commitment and engagement levels, quality of relationship with management, and system barriers to performance) as part of the performance coaching conversation. In your planning for the coaching conversation you may have identified a number of process goals to discuss during the conversation, and this is the time to shift the focus of the coaching conversation toward these goals.

Here is a list of some possible questions you can ask the employee in order to explore these crucial process goals:

- What do you find most rewarding and satisfying about this job?
- How engaged are you in doing the work that you do every day? Do you find the work meaningful? If so, in what way? If not, why not? What inspires you, or what holds you back?
- Where do you see yourself five years from now? Where would you like to be in your career with this company? What skill or knowledge training would you like to pursue to advance your career goals here?
- Talk to me about how connected you feel to this organization? Is this an organization you would encourage your family and friends to work for? Why or why not?

- How comfortable do you feel with the quality of our working relationship? Do you feel that you can approach me with questions and issues at any time? Am I available when you need me? Do you have confidence that I am working to help you be successful here?

- How could I be most helpful to you in achieving your performance goals?

- What are the system barriers that sometimes get in the way of your ability to do the job? To what extent do the organization's policies and practices enable or undermine your success?

- To what extent is our work area or team helpful to you in moving toward your performance success?

The point of asking these questions during the coaching conversation is to open up a dialogue with the employee that gets at the heart of the employee's level of engagement and the quality of the relationship that the employee has with you. While the main focus of the coaching conversation—as we stated earlier—needs to be on the employee's outcome goals, the employee's level of engagement and his relationship with you do influence whether the outcome goals will be achieved. So, after you've discussed the employee's performance strengths and areas for improvement and developed a number of outcome goals, it's crucial that you invest time toward the end of your conversation in discussing ways to strengthen the employee's engagement levels and your performance partnership.

Working from a collaborative mindset, you are genuinely curious about how engaged the employee is with his daily work and with the organization, and you want to understand how the employee perceives the relationship that he has with you. You are open to hearing what the employee has to say, and you explore the thinking and reasoning behind what he is saying. Because one of your goals as a coach should include strengthening employee engagement and building a strong working partnership with the employee, we believe that you need to make this segment of the coaching conversation a meaningful dialogue that leads to insight and learning for both of you.

Finally, we believe that you need to make time within your coaching conversation to discuss broad system barriers or obstacles that may be limiting the employee's performance success. Some system obstacles may have already been identified during your discussion of the employee's performance challenges and the causes behind these challenges. Other system obstacles, however, may be influencing the employee's performance in general and, as the employee's performance coach, it's important that you become aware of these. For this reason, we think that it's important to ask the employee questions about possible system barriers such as the organization's policies and practices, quality of the working relationships on the team, quality of the organization's learning and development program, quality and timeliness of information systems that provide performance data to the employee, clarity and resonance of the organization's strategic priorities and goals, and effectiveness of organizational communications.

Surfacing the employee's perceptions of possible system barriers and together discussing these potential obstacles to the employee's performance success allow you to better understand what the employee views as system challenges. It also enables you to explore with the employee ideas and strategies for working around these organizational barriers. Lastly, the employee may surface system barriers that require more than an employee workaround. Addressing such situations may require a concerted effort by you and other managers. If, for example, one or more employees identify that the organization's learning and development program isn't offering programs or opportunities relevant to their jobs, then it may be up to you and your fellow managers to approach the human resource development office about these concerns.

At the conclusion of this phase of the performance coaching conversation you and the employee will have a better understanding of the employee's engagement levels, your performance partnership, and any system barriers to the employee's performance. You will also have mutually developed some goals that both of you might contribute to in order to help support the employee's future performance success.

Summarizing Areas of Mutual Agreement

As the summary performance coaching conversation winds down, it's time to bring together the ideas, issues, and goals that you've mutually discussed by having each of you summarize what you have committed to do to support the employee's current performance, improve performance, move performance to a new level or in a new direction, strengthen the employee's engagement, invest in your performance partnership, and address system barriers. Here's our recommended sequence for summarizing what you've both agreed to do.

Summarize Key Next Steps

Invite the employee to summarize his understanding of the conclusions and actions that you have both agreed to as a result of this coaching conversation. Reinforce those understandings and expectations that agree with yours and seek clarification from the employee if and when you have a different understanding of what you've both agreed to. Identify additional areas where understanding is still needed, if appropriate, and verify his understanding of these additional areas.

Reiterate Mutual Agreement

Offer a reiteration of the mutual agreement that both of you have achieved as you understand it. Summarize the actions each of you has committed to take to improve, enhance, and sustain high levels of performance for the future. Ensure that you include in your summary what specifically each of you will keep doing or do differently to support and enable the employee's great performance. Ask the employee if your summary sounds about right or if you missed any-thing critical.

Discuss Next Steps

If appropriate, indicate that your next step will be to finalize the for-mal performance review form based upon today's discussion and that you would like to schedule another meeting—much briefer this time—to discuss the employee's final performance rating and any pay-related implications. Reiterate that the conversation has been helpful—that it's given you a better understanding of the employee's performance. Indicate that your final assessment and final overall rat-ing of the employee's performance will reflect what you learned in this discussion and what each of you have agreed to do for the future.

Offer the Employee Assistance Program or Explore a Reasonable Accommodation of a Disability if Warranted

If you suspect that there may be a personal problem behind any of the employee's performance issues that you explored during the coaching conversation, do *not* state your suspicions! Instead, we rec-ommend that you say to the employee:

> *If these performance challenges that we've discussed today are a result of personal problems that you may be experiencing, you might find that our organization's employee assistance program may be helpful. Here is the contact information for our EAP.*

You'll also want to note that EAP provides free and confidential assistance upon request. Explain that your reason for offering the EAP is based upon your desire to enable him to be successful in this job and that you are not presuming that the employee has a personal problem.

If you suspect that the employee may have a physical, mental, or emotional disability that impairs the employee's ability to perform his job, we recommend that you take some time during the conversa-tion to review with the employee whether there are any medical or disability barriers affecting his performance. Ideally, you've already explored this possibility with human resources, and, therefore, you have a good sense of how to raise this issue with the employee. If the employee expresses interest in exploring this issue further, you can then encourage the employee to request an evaluation and, if warranted, a reasonable accommodation.

Schedule the Next Performance Coaching Conversation

We think that it's a good idea for you and the employee to discuss and establish a follow-along schedule for future check-in performance coaching conversations. Developing a roadmap for these future check-in conversations allows the two of you to stay connected and on the same page in terms of expectations, measuring results, taking corrective action, problem solving, and strengthening the relationship. Ongoing check-in coaching conversations also provide you both with an opportunity to discuss additional support the employee may need to achieve star-level performance.

Conclusion

We recommend that you end the summary performance coaching conversation by again expressing appreciation for the employee's performance and the employee's commitment to great performance in the future. We think that it's useful to reiterate how helpful the conversation has been at enabling you to understand how best to support the employee's future performance. If desired, indicate that you will be following up on this meeting with an e-mail or memo summarizing what you both have agreed upon. Alternatively, you might invite the employee to take the lead role in summarizing what you've each agreed to do as a result of this conversation and then forwarding a copy to you.

Following Up and Following Through

Whew! You did it! Using the tools that we introduced in this book and especially leaning upon the values, assumptions, and enacting behaviors of the collaborative mindset, you successfully charted your way through your first summary performance coaching conversation. If it went well, you and the employee engaged in a meaningful dialogue about the employee's performance and about how you, in your coaching role, can be most helpful in supporting the employee's future performance. Fear was pushed to the margins as you invited the employee to take a lead role in the assessment process, and you listened with an open mind as the employee offered his view of his performance behaviors and outcomes. Each of you learned something about the other and yourself during the conversation, and, most importantly, the two of you mutually developed a suite of outcome and process goals that will help translate the insights from the coaching conversation into great results in the next performance period.

In your role as a coach, you have a few things you still need to do following the conversation:

- Follow through in addressing the training, information, equipment, and other organizational support needs that were identified during the conversation.

- Observe the employee in action, and reinforce positive behaviors and outcomes when you see them. When a performance problem arises, bring up the issue immediately. Don't wait until the next formal performance coaching conversation to let the employee know that he is on the right track or that there's a performance issue that needs addressing.

- Continue tracking performance outcomes, gathering performance data, and documenting results in performance logs and in the employee's performance portfolio.

- Reward any degree of performance improvement. Reinforce all positive behaviors and outcomes—as long as they are moving the employee toward his performance goals.

And finally, make sure that you continue to invest in ongoing check-in performance coaching conversations as needed to discuss the employee's progress. If called for due to new and emerging performance issues, priorities, initiatives, challenges, and so forth, check-in coaching conversations can be used to identify new performance expectations and directions—which gives you and the employee the opportunity to renegotiate the employee's performance goals as required.

Next Steps for Ensuring Fearless Reviews Today and Tomorrow

We've covered a lot of ground in this book. In Chapter 1 we discussed the origins of the fear that is common in performance reviews. We explored the my-way mindset in Chapters 2 through 4, and then in Chapters 5 through 9 we discussed the collaborative mindset. In Chapters 10 through 13 we guided you into a new framework for understanding performance (the great performance management cycle) and provided strategies for understanding causation of exemplary and mediocre performance and laying a foundation for success. We've touched on what we believe are the core elements for transforming fear-inducing performance reviews into powerful performance coaching conversations. Making this journey from the traditional approach to this more conversational and two-way approach won't be without its challenges, but, if you find a way to embrace the collaborative mindset in your role as a supervisor and coach, we think that you'll find this path surprisingly easy to walk.

We hope that you will find our roadmap to this new terrain useful as you work with both your star performers and those who are in the process of becoming star performers. And if you find yourself frustrated and angry with an employee—just like supervisor Tom in the story we introduced to you in Chapter 1—we hope that you (1) acknowledge your frustration and anger; (2) identify why you are feeling this way and how these emotions influence your thinking, assumptions, and judgments about the employee; and then (3) reconnect with the values and enacting behaviors of the collaborative mindset to focus yourself on empathy, understanding, openness to different viewpoints, and the insight and learning that will inevitably emerge. You might end up being right about the "wayward" employee who is causing all of your angst, and it may indeed be time to help the person "find his happiness elsewhere." But at least you've driven fear into the background and made an attempt to make things work out with your employee.

Good luck in the next steps in your journey!

APPENDIX A

PERFORMANCE COACHING CONVERSATION PREPARATION GUIDE

Reflect back upon the past three months, six months, or year and explore your work performance and outcomes as you consider the following questions.

What is going well with the job and why is it going well? What about the job is working? What are some of the good things that are happening in each of your job responsibility areas? What recent accomplishments are you especially proud of? What parts of your job do you feel especially good about? Are there any strength areas where you could further raise the bar on your performance? Why is the job or this aspect of the job going well?

What isn't going well in the job? What aspects of your job aren't working as well as you'd like? What job problems or difficulties in any of your responsibility areas have you experienced lately?

Why isn't this going well? What are the likely causes of performance challenges? If you are experiencing performance challenges, what might be the *causes* of these things not going well?

What changes or improvements could you make in how you approach your job to help you maintain areas where you are strong, move your performance to a new level, or improve things that are not going well? What actions could you take that would enable you to sustain your performance where things are going well? What could you do to build upon your past success and move your performance to a new level? What actions could you take to address the causes of things not going well and which, if you took these actions, would likely improve your future performance outcomes and goals?

How might I (your supervisor) help you to be more successful in your job? What can I do more or less of to enable you to achieve or exceed your performance goals?

What do you see as performance areas where there may be a need for new responsibilities and future growth in your performance? Based upon what you see going on in the organization and in your job, what new directions do you see your position moving in? What new responsibilities should be added to your position in the future? Which responsibilities are *less* important now than previously? How do you see your job changing over the next performance period?

Additional Questions for the More Formal Summary Performance Coaching Conversation:

How would you assess your overall performance and your performance for each of your job and organizational responsibilities? For each responsibility area, to what extent are you exceeding, meeting, or failing to meet your performance goals? What measures are you using to gauge your performance in each area? What factors are supporting or limiting your success in each of these areas?

What are your long-term professional development and career goals? Where do you see yourself five years from now? What's most important to you in your work? What would you most like to accomplish in your work here?

Appendix B

Common Questions and Answers About Fearless Performance Reviews

*F*earless *Performance Reviews* offers a powerful framework for strengthening the performance partnership between managers and employees and lays down a solid foundation for preparing for and navigating the performance coaching conversation to ensure a truly fearless review. We are confident that you can apply our approach to your own performance reviews and find a way to integrate our ideas and strategies into your process. The final pages of this book strive to support the application of our approach into real-world performance reviews. Over the years our clients have asked us a variety of practical questions about how to build these ideas into their performance management practices, and we thought it would be useful to share these questions and our answers with you.

Here are some of the most frequently asked questions about our approach and our responses.

How often should the performance coaching conversation be conducted?

The best response to this question is as often as necessary. We carefully consider several variables when determining the frequency of coaching conversations: What is the competence and confidence level of the employee? How much change is occurring in the performance environment? Is the employee generally performing well, or is he struggling? Are there frequent interactions between you and the employee where you get to observe and discuss performance issues—or are these opportunities to observe and discuss performance infrequent?

Based upon the answers to these questions, the manager and employee would mutually determine the most useful frequency for conducting performance coaching conversations. In circumstances when the amount of change in the performance environment is significant, when there are lower levels of employee competence and confidence, or when the employee is struggling, there is a need for greater frequency of these coaching conversations.

The traditional once-a-year assessment is simply insufficient to facilitate the desired level of continuous employee insight, learning, and development. Minimally, we recommend that the more formal *summary* performance coaching conversation (with all of the associated performance analysis and planning we discussed in this book) be conducted at least twice a year—with more frequent and less formal coaching conversations interspersed between the more formal conversations. The less structured conversations are conducted as needed to keep both the manager and employee connected regarding performance expectations, results, challenges, opportunities, and so forth. Since the goal of these less formal coaching conversations is to facilitate the flow of information and to strengthen the partnership between the manager and the employee, they generally don't require the deeper performance assessment and planning that accompany the more formal performance coaching conversation.

When you increase the frequency of the interactions between the manager and the employee through both the more formal performance coaching conversation and the less formal coaching conversation, you increase the opportunities for guiding the employee toward performance improvement. If our goal is to facilitate employee insight, learning, and performance improvement, then we need to increase the frequency of all forms of the coaching conversation.

How does the performance coaching conversation—and this entire approach—interact with discipline and termination?

Discipline including its most extreme form, termination of employment, are entirely separate from the performance coaching conversation process. The goal of the performance coaching conversation is to guide an employee toward maintaining, improving, building upon, or shifting the focus of her performance. The goal of discipline is to get an employee to immediately stop an undesirable behavior or performance level and direct the employee toward a more desirable performance behavior or outcome.

The manager uses the performance coaching conversation to create a shared understanding with the employee regarding where the employee's performance is currently and what both the employee and the manager may need to do to maintain or enhance the employee's performance. With discipline, the manager uses the prospect of imposing increasingly negative sanctions to get the employee's attention and to compel the employee to do the right thing to achieve the right results.

Discipline often occurs when the gap between performance expectations and performance results is large enough and sustained long enough such that it can no longer be tolerated by the organization. Managers can often decrease the need for discipline by increasing the frequency of both the formal summary performance coaching conversation as well as the less formal "check-in" performance coaching conversations. If the manager and employee are staying connected and maintaining their shared understanding of performance expectations and results, there will be less need for discipline since an employee's performance gap should never become unacceptably large due to the frequent conversations about what's working and what's not. By discussing an employee's undesirable or inappropriate behaviors or performance early on and exploring ideas and strategies for changing the employee's behaviors or results, discipline can often be avoided.

The performance coaching conversation should always precede any disciplinary process. Having meaningful conversations about performance expectations and results, the underlying causes of performance challenges, and mutually exploring ideas and strategies for closing performance gaps should lead to both stronger performance outcomes and a stronger performance partnership. If the undesirable behaviors continue or performance doesn't improve, however, it may be necessary to shift from coaching conversations to progressive discipline where there is a gradual increasing of negative outcomes or sanctions. While even with discipline managers continue to pursue a shared understanding about expectations, underlying causes of performance problems, and ideas for solving performance gaps, the threat of sanctions makes it much harder for the employee to maintain a focus on insight, learning, growth, and development.

A major downside of using discipline is that it often shifts everyone's mindset from one based upon collaboration toward the more counterproductive my-may unilateralist approach. As we discussed in this book, the my-way mindset is often driven by fear and leads people to engage in defensive and self-protective behaviors—neither of which facilitates insight and learning in the employee or the manager. For this reason, our goal should always be to use the collaborative mindset to inform our coaching conversations and to only use discipline as a last resort. For, once we begin using discipline—even a level of discipline with minimal sanctions—our actions are likely to be perceived as a threat, which will often lead to the defensive strategies of the my-way mindset and may actually reduce the employee's receptivity to new ideas and learning.

Progressive discipline does get people's attention and can lead to performance improvement. It's a strategy that you may need to use to let an employee know that you are serious about his behaviors or performance. Sometimes it's the best approach for letting employees know that things have to change or there will be negative consequences. It should never, however, be our lead strategy. Start with the performance coaching conversation within the framework of the collaborative mindset.

What's the best way to integrate peer evaluations or some form of 360-degree assessment into the performance coaching conversation?

As we discussed in this book, it's important that performance reviews and performance coaching conversations are based upon a comprehensive and holistic understanding of the employee's performance. For this reason, we think that finding ways to integrate the perspectives of peers, customers, or others with whom the employee interacts into the performance coaching conversation is a good idea.

We offer you several different approaches for gathering peer or other feedback. In all cases, however, the process begins with the manager and employee agreeing upon a list of three to five peers, customers, or other key stakeholders from whom receiving feedback on the employee's performance would be helpful. We recommend that the employee initiate this process by identifying several names and then the manager responding to this list by either approving the list or offering additions or substitutions. The final result should be a list of people who know the employee's work well and who can be trusted to provide honest and objective feedback on the employee's performance.

Once you have a list of potential feedback providers, the next step is to identify the set of questions to explore. Regardless of the methodology that you use (which we will soon address), here are the broad questions to explore:

Considering your interactions with the employee over the past 3, 4, 6, or 12 months, please respond to the following:

1. **Assets:** Thinking about your working relationship with this person, what are the employee's performance assets or strengths? What does he do very well? What do you value most about this person's performance contributions?

2. **Improvement Areas:** Where could this employee most improve? Where could he do better in relation to his work with you?

3. **Actions to Leverage Talents and Reduce Barriers:** Actions the employee could take to best leverage his talents and reduce barriers to performance include ...

4. **New Ways to Maximize Value:** How might this employee serve you or work with you in new ways that would maximize his value to you in the future? What new performance directions should this employee pursue to further enhance his value to you and others?

Here are a few approaches for integrating peer evaluations or others' viewpoints that we would recommend—each approach using the agreed-upon list of peers or others to provide feedback:

- The employee or supervisor sends an e-mail or memo to the feedback providers asking them to complete and return the feedback form that explores some version of the questions listed above. The form would be forwarded to the manager.

- The employee sends an e-mail or memo to the feedback providers asking them to complete and return the feedback form that explores some version of the questions listed above. The form would be forwarded to the employee who would then integrate the feedback into his own self-assessment. The employee would then forward the feedback forms to his manager.

- A 360-degree feedback process involves the employee or manager distributing online surveys to respondents, asking them to complete the feedback survey. The data is automatically compiled by the online 360-degree assessment system, and the report is shared with the employee and his manager. The 360-degree survey can mirror the four open-ended questions above and could also examine specific performance dimensions in greater detail using a scaled frequency response.

- Following the collection of the survey data, the employee could meet with the feedback providers to explore their comments in order to better understand the data and integrate it into the his self-assessment.

Our company uses an intranet-based system for performance reviews where the employee's self-assessment and the manager's review are both done online. What's the best way to integrate this online process with the face-to-face performance coaching conversation that you propose in this book?

When used in the right way, online-based performance management systems can be powerful tools to assist both the employee and the manager with the performance feedback process. The online tools can be efficient ways to document performance data as well as the results of performance conversations. Many of these online systems have mechanisms by which the employee conducts a performance self-assessment using the same evaluation criteria that is used by the manager.

We believe that online performance management systems are most effective when they make it easy for the employee and manager to document performance issues throughout the year. When things are easier, people will tend to use them more frequently. And, when it comes to documenting performance issues, increasing the frequency helps contribute to a more meaningful, data-based system for documenting performance.

A good online system for documenting and even evaluating employee performance can serve as a great foundation for performance management, but it is no substitute for the actual face-to-face performance coaching conversation. The online process should support, not replace, the rich interaction that can only come when the employee and manager sit down and explore the employee's past and future performance.

A number of the online performance management systems involve both employee self-assessments and collecting feedback from others (e.g., peers, customers, and stakeholders). When and how these data are shared with the employee and the manager are important. The survey data received from others can be powerful drivers for the employee's self-assessment and to help the manager gain a more holistic understanding of the employee's performance. Performance feedback from others should be shared with both the employee and the manager prior to the employee's online self-assessment and the manager's online assessment of the employee.

We believe, however, that the employee's online self-assessment should not be shared with the manager before the manager completes her own assessment of the employee's performance. If the manager reads the employee's self-assessment before completing her own assessment of the employee's performance, the manager's viewpoint is likely to be influenced by the employee's self-assessment. We think it's crucial that the manager complete her own assessment of the employee's performance first and then review the employee's self-assessment rather than writing the employee review based upon or in reaction to the employee's self-assessment. The manager is still able to make adjustments to her review of the employee's performance that reflects the employee's self-assessment, but the core of the manager's assessment is based upon her objective and independent judgment of the employee's work.

As we discussed earlier in this book, the goal of an effective performance management process is using objective performance data to drive a meaningful dialogue between the manager and the employee such that the employee's future performance is strengthened. To the extent that these online performance management systems support this outcome, they can add significant value to the process. But, if these online systems become a substitute for the dialogue or if they undermine the objectivity of the manager's viewpoint, then the employee and manager need to make adjustments to how they will use the system to ensure that it enhances, not under-mines, the desired outcomes.

How should I utilize this process alongside our existing performance review forms? In addition, our review form includes a final rating scale that asks me to give a final assessment of the employee's performance (e.g., exceeds expectations, meets expectations, fails to meet expectations, needs improvement). I've found this to be pretty discouraging to employees. How do I prevent the final assessment rating from becoming the focus of the performance coaching conversation and distracting the employee from insights, learning, and growth?

Our approach to performance management and the performance coaching conversation can be used with any existing performance management system. The key is to adhere to the goals of an effective process and a meaningful dialogue while also respecting the processes and forms that your organization uses. At the same time, the performance review forms used by your organization should never get in the way of the performance coaching conversation. And, if they are getting in the way of the conversation, then you may need to be creative in how you integrate the forms with the conversation.

One of our concerns with many performance review forms is that they ask the manager to use various ratings scales to offer a judgment of the employee's performance effectiveness on individual performance dimensions and, usually, a summary judgment of the employee's over-all performance. To the extent that these rating scales are behavior-ally anchored or cite specific and measurable performance outcomes, they can be an effective mechanism to provide helpful feedback to the employee. Unfortunately, these scales often lack specificity or don't reflect objective measures (e.g., fails to meet expectations, meets expectations), and, unless they are accompanied by a supporting nar-rative that provides sufficient objective performance documentation, the rating scales just get in the way of the conversation. They become a barrier to the conversation because the employee tends to zero in on the rating rather than on insight and learning that evolve from the coaching conversation.

To address this problem, we recommend that the manager leave the various checkbox scales blank and hold off discussing the form until near the end of the coaching conversation. The coaching conversation should never be about the form, but the form can be a useful way to integrate and summarize key performance issues and to ensure that the conversation has touched on all relevant performance dimensions. As the performance coaching conversation winds down the manager should explain that the next step in the process is for him to take the next several days to reflect upon the conversation that they've just had and then to integrate the resulting insights and goals into the official form. The manager will note that the two of them will then hold a brief follow-along session to review the finalized form, discuss the final ratings, and then sign and submit the form to human resources.

Before the follow-along session, the manager revises the performance review form to reflect insights from the performance coaching conversation and then checks the boxes on each of the rating scales, ensuring that the boxes checked reflect objective and data-based perspectives. During the follow-along session with the employee the focus is no longer on the conversation and is therefore less interested in exploring new insights and learning. As a result, in this final session the focus shifts to sharing the completed form, providing a mechanism for the employee to offer written feedback or a response to the manager's rating scale selections, and getting the employee's signature.

By keeping the focus on the conversation in the first meeting and shifting to the official form toward the end of the conversation and in the follow-along meeting, we believe that managers can have fearless performance reviews while honoring their organization's performance evaluation forms.

Finally, if the form your company uses continue to be a major stumbling block to effective performance coaching conversations, we encourage you to contact human resources and advocate for a change in the form. Rather than construct creative work-arounds that may or may not work, why not become a catalyst to change the form to reflect a better process? If that's the path you choose to walk, we encourage you to use some of the approaches contained in this book to help transform your process.

This whole process depends upon the employee stepping up and taking a proactive and leading role in her performance management and performance review. What if I try this employee-centered performance coaching conversation and the employee simply doesn't say anything or fails to conduct a thorough self-assessment?

In our experience, most employees respond very well to the idea of taking the lead role in the performance assessment process. They appreciate the opportunity to use their self-assessment as the foundation of the process and the chance to take the lead role in exploring and addressing barriers to great performance. It's also our experience that this isn't true for some employees. For a wide variety of reasons, some employees are unable or unwilling to step up into a lead role in their performance assessment or during the performance coaching conversation.

When employees display reluctance to take a more active role in the process, our first question is, why? What's holding the employee back from full ownership of this process? Depending upon the cause, the way forward for the manager may be different. Here are our thoughts on actions the manager can take to increase employee engagement depending upon the cause behind the lack of engagement and ownership:

• The employee does not fully understanding what taking a
  lead role in the process means. Once the manager verifies this

as the likely cause of the employee's failing to be engaged in the process, the manager may need to have a preassessment conversation that introduces or revisits the idea of employee ownership of the performance management process and what this looks like. Discussing why employee ownership of the process matters and how this level of employee ownership translates into the employee taking a lead role by conducting a meaningful self-assessment is crucial in order for the employee to know what is expected of him in the process.

- The employee is not skilled in self-assessment. Once the manager verifies this cause, he or she may need to model the process by asking a series of questions that guide the employee in reflecting upon her performance. While such a question-based approach should essentially mirror the format of the performance coaching conversation, we envision the manager using a more active approach to guide the employee in self-reflection in advance of the coaching conversation. Helping the employee develop the skills of critical thinking and self-assessment may take extensive behavioral modeling and managerial support, but, over time, an employee who is open to the idea of self-assessment but simply not skilled at it is likely to become more proficient at it.

- The employee does not care enough about ownership or does not take the process seriously. Once the manager verifies this possible cause with the employee, she may need to reemphasize the value to both the employee and the manager of the employee taking the lead role. When the employee doesn't have answers to the manager's questions (e.g., What's going well? What's not going well? What are the causes of what's going well and not well?), the manager might suggest rescheduling the performance coaching conversation to give the employee more time to reflect upon her performance and to prepare for the conversation. By stopping the conversation and suggesting rescheduling, the manager is saying that she is serious about the employee's active involvement and that she expects the employee to take it seriously as well.

- The employee is fearful of speaking truthfully about performance challenges because of the potential implications of identifying these challenges. Once the manager verifies this possible cause with the employee, the manager may need to spend more time talking about the value of accurate self-assessment, how accurate self-assessment is a reflection of the employee's ability to engage in critical reflection, and how valuable this skill is to the manager. The most powerful way for a manager to reduce this fear is by demonstrating genuine interest in and appreciation for the employee surfacing performance issues and challenges early rather than later. Praising critical self-assessment, thanking the employee for bringing these issues forward, and shifting from the performance challenges to exploring possible solutions are a few of the strategies that a manager might use to help diffuse employee anxiety about surfacing performance challenges.

This whole process seems as if it would take a lot of work and a lot of time. Given the number of people I supervise, I don't have time to do this for each of my employees. If I were to conduct this level of analysis for each of my direct reports and then have to schedule two meetings with each employee (one for the basic conversation and another for the discussion of pay implications), I wouldn't have time for anything else!

We hear this a lot: what you are proposing will double the time I put into this process, and I don't have enough time to do it effectively now! Our position is that by making this process an employee-centered one the total time requirements for the manager will actually decrease. Instead of taking the lead role in the process—which, in the traditional review, involves writing up the evaluation and completing the form in advance of the review—the manager looks to the employee to take a lead role in presenting his performance analysis and in offering strategies and solutions for moving performance to a new level. Yes, the manager still does the necessary preassessment analysis and puts sufficient time into preparations so that she goes into the assessment with a set of goals for the session, but the burden of carrying the process is shared if not largely shifted to the employee.

So, instead of taking an hour or more to write up the employee's evaluation prior to the performance coaching conversation, the manager will do some analysis, make some notes (as extensive as she wishes), and then go into the conversation with an openness to learning from the employee. Then, following the conversation, the manager can be far more time efficient by summarizing the results from the conversation on the final review form. The manager spends less time trying to guess at causation of problems or to invent solutions to performance challenges and more time simply documenting what the two of them discussed during the performance coaching conversation.

We don't envision that the recommended follow-along meeting where the manager's final assessment is presented and the official form is completed and signed will be a very long or intensive meeting. Since generally this follow-along meeting isn't about discovery or problem solving but is instead focused on affirming and bringing closure to what was discussed at the performance coaching conversation, we see this meeting as being quite brief.

Finally, the larger purpose of our approach to performance management, the collaborative mindset, and the performance coaching conversation is to build a shared understanding of expectations and performance results and to strengthen the relationship between the manager and the employee. When these things are accomplished, we think that there will be much less time spent by both the manager and the employee solving performance problems, putting out fires, having meetings about performance and not addressing the root causes of problems, and so forth. As the saying goes, "pay me now, or pay me later." The opportunity and time costs for not making the right time investments at the front end will inevitably lead to wasted time down the road.

By ensuring that employees are on the right path, self-managing as they travel that path, and sharing information with the manager when problems and challenges arise, this process is destined to enable higher employee productivity and quality. This, in turn, leads to less managerial time spent on fixing things that aren't right and less time in the office of human resources trying to figure out how to get rid of an underperforming employee.

Notes

Introduction

1. Oxford Dictionaries, online edition.
2. Ibid.

Chapter 6

1. Jalāl ad-Dīn Muhammad Rūmī, 1207–1273.

Chapter 8

1. Plato, *The Apology of Socrates*, 28c.

Chapter 10

1. Van Der Zee, Han. *Measuring the Value of Information Technology.* Hershey, PA: IRM Press, 2003, 5.
2. Thorndike, E. L. "A constant error on psychological rating." *Journal of Applied Psychology,* IV (1920): 25–29.

Chapter 11

1. The origins of our definition of *great performance* come from concepts outlined in the book *Flight of the Buffalo* by James Belasco and Ralph Stayer (1993).

Chapter 12

1. Rosenthal, Robert & Jacobson, Lenore. *Pygmalion in the classroom* (Expanded ed.). New York: Irvington, 1992.

2. Russell, Jeffrey and Linda. "Engage Your Workforce." *ASTD Press Infoline*, Vol 27, Issue 1004 (2010).

INDEX

About the Authors

Jeffrey and Linda Russell are the founders and codirectors of Russell Consulting, Inc., headquartered in Madison, Wisconsin (www.RussellConsultingInc.com). For more than 20 years, Russell Consulting has provided consulting and training services in leadership, strategic thinking and planning, leading change, employee engagement surveys, organizational development, performance coaching, and performance management. Their diverse list of clients includes Fortune 500 companies, small businesses, social and nonprofit organizations, and government agencies.

Jeff's bachelor of arts in humanism and cultural change and master of arts in industrial relations are both from the University of Wisconsin. He serves as an adjunct faculty member for the University of Wisconsin, teaching for the Small Business Development Center, the Wisconsin Certified Public Manager Program, and a number of other certification programs with University of Wisconsin campuses. Jeff is a frequent presenter at local, state, regional, and international conferences.

Linda's bachelor of arts is in social work from the University of Wisconsin. She has completed graduate work in rehabilitation counseling, also at the University of Wisconsin. Linda specializes in designing and implementing job-engagement and quality-of-worklife surveys and in facilitating team and organizational development interventions.

Jeff and Linda together have authored nine other books including *Leading Change Training* (ASTD Press, 2003), *Strategic Planning Training* (ASTD Press, 2005), *Change Basics* (ASTD Press, 2006), and *Ultimate*

Performance Management (ASTD Press, 2009). They also periodically publish *Workplace Enhancement Notes,* a journal of tips for leading great organizations.

Within their vision to help leaders create and sustain great organizations, Russell Consulting, Inc. integrates theory, research, and real-world experience in its consulting and training practice. Jeff and Linda help their clients find practical solutions in a world that too often offers strategies that are long on hype and short on substance.

Readers who want to know more about Jeff and Linda and their work or want to subscribe to their workplace journal are encouraged to visit them at www.RussellConsultingInc.com or to send them an e-mail at RCI@RussellConsultingInc.com. Please contact them with questions about the ideas presented in this book or to learn more about RCI's consulting or training services.